Grand Canyon Trivia Trek

Grand Canyon Trivia Trek

An Intrepid Rim-to-Rim Historical Journey

Flood Hefley

JOHNSON BOOKS
BOULDER

Published by Johnson Books
a Big Earth Publishing company
3005 Center Green Drive, Suite 225, Boulder, Colorado 80301
1-800-258-5830
E-mail: books@bigearthpublishing.com
www.bigearthpublishing.com

Cover and text design by Rebecca Finkel
Cover photos by Flood Hefley. Clockwise from left:
Havasu Falls; Grand View Fire Lookout Tower, South Rim; Mules on the North Kaibab Trail;
view of Wotans Throne from the North Rim at Cape Royal

9 8 7 6 5 4

Library of Congress Cataloging-in-Publication Data
Hefley, Flood.
Grand Canyon trivia trek / Flood Hefley.
p. cm.
ISBN 978-1-55566-430-5
1. Grand Canyon National Park (Ariz.)—History.
2. Grand Canyon National Park (Ariz.)—Miscellanea. I. Title.
F788.H46 2010
979.1'32—dc22 2010000206

Printed in the United States of America

For my wife Kathleen and my kids
and Fred "Andy" Anderson,
my Grand Canyon mentor

In memory of
my mom, Selma,
who encouraged me
to keep a
Grand Canyon journal

Contents

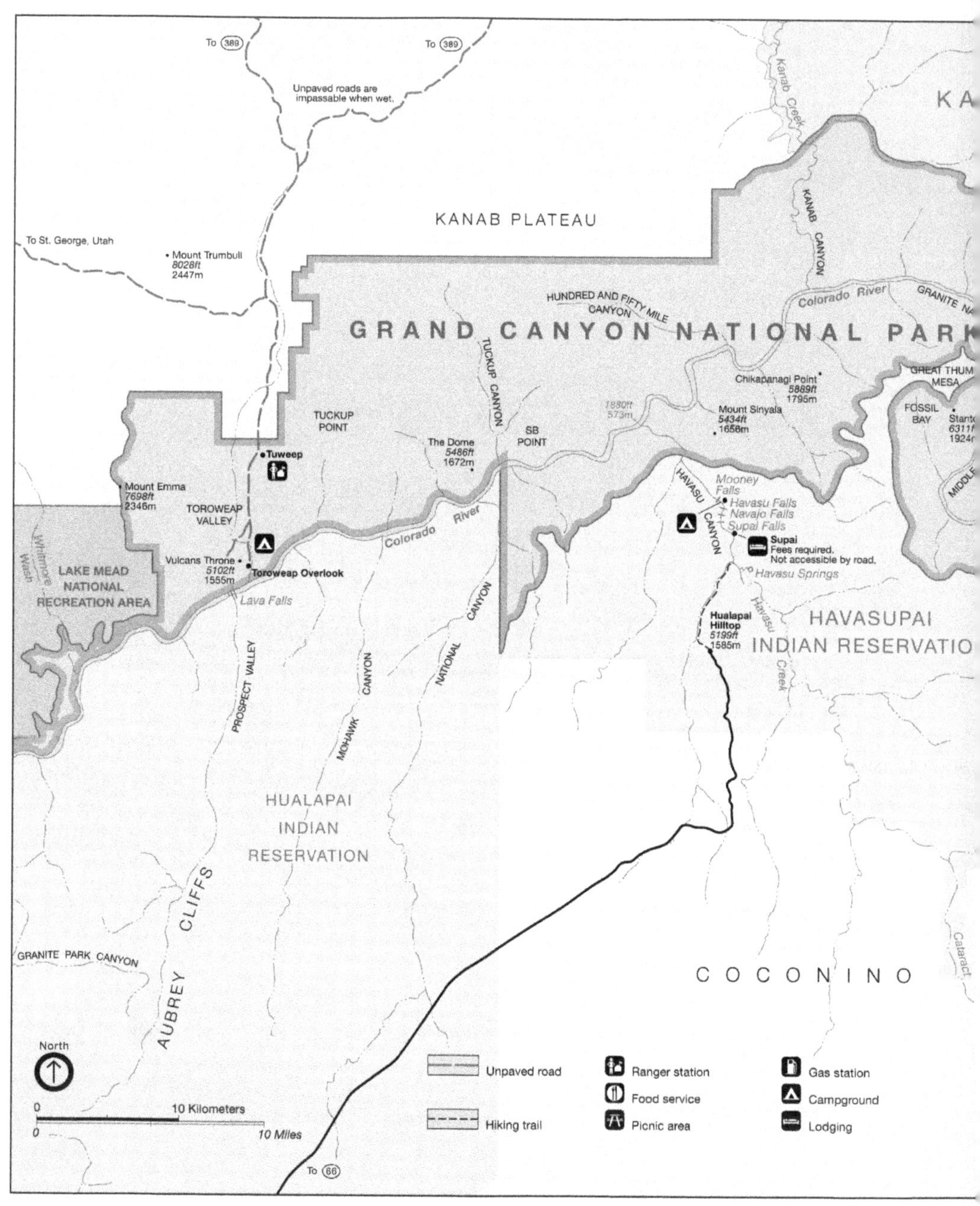
To 389
To 389
Unpaved roads are impassable when wet.
KANAB PLATEAU
To St. George, Utah
Mount Trumbull 8028ft 2447m
Kanab Creek
KANAB CANYON
HUNDRED AND FIFTY MILE CANYON
Colorado River
GRANITE NA
GRAND CANYON NATIONAL PARK
TUCKUP CANYON
GREAT THUMB MESA
Chikapanagi Point 5889ft 1795m
TUCKUP POINT
1880ft 573m
Mount Sinyala 5434ft 1656m
FOSSIL BAY
The Dome 5486ft 1672m
SB POINT
Tuweep
Mount Emma 7698ft 2346m
TOROWEAP VALLEY
HAVASU CANYON
Mooney Falls
Havasu Falls
Navajo Falls
Supai Falls
Supai
Fees required.
Not accessible by road.
Havasu Springs
Whitmore Wash
LAKE MEAD NATIONAL RECREATION AREA
Vulcans Throne 5102ft 1555m
Toroweap Overlook
Lava Falls
Colorado River
Hualapai Hilltop 5199ft 1585m
HAVASUPAI INDIAN RESERVATIO
Havasu Creek
PROSPECT VALLEY
MOHAWK CANYON
NATIONAL CANYON
HUALAPAI INDIAN RESERVATION
GRANITE PARK CANYON
AUBREY CLIFFS
COCONINO
Cataract
North
0 10 Kilometers
0 10 Miles
To 66
Unpaved road
Hiking trail
Ranger station
Food service
Picnic area
Gas station
Campground
Lodging

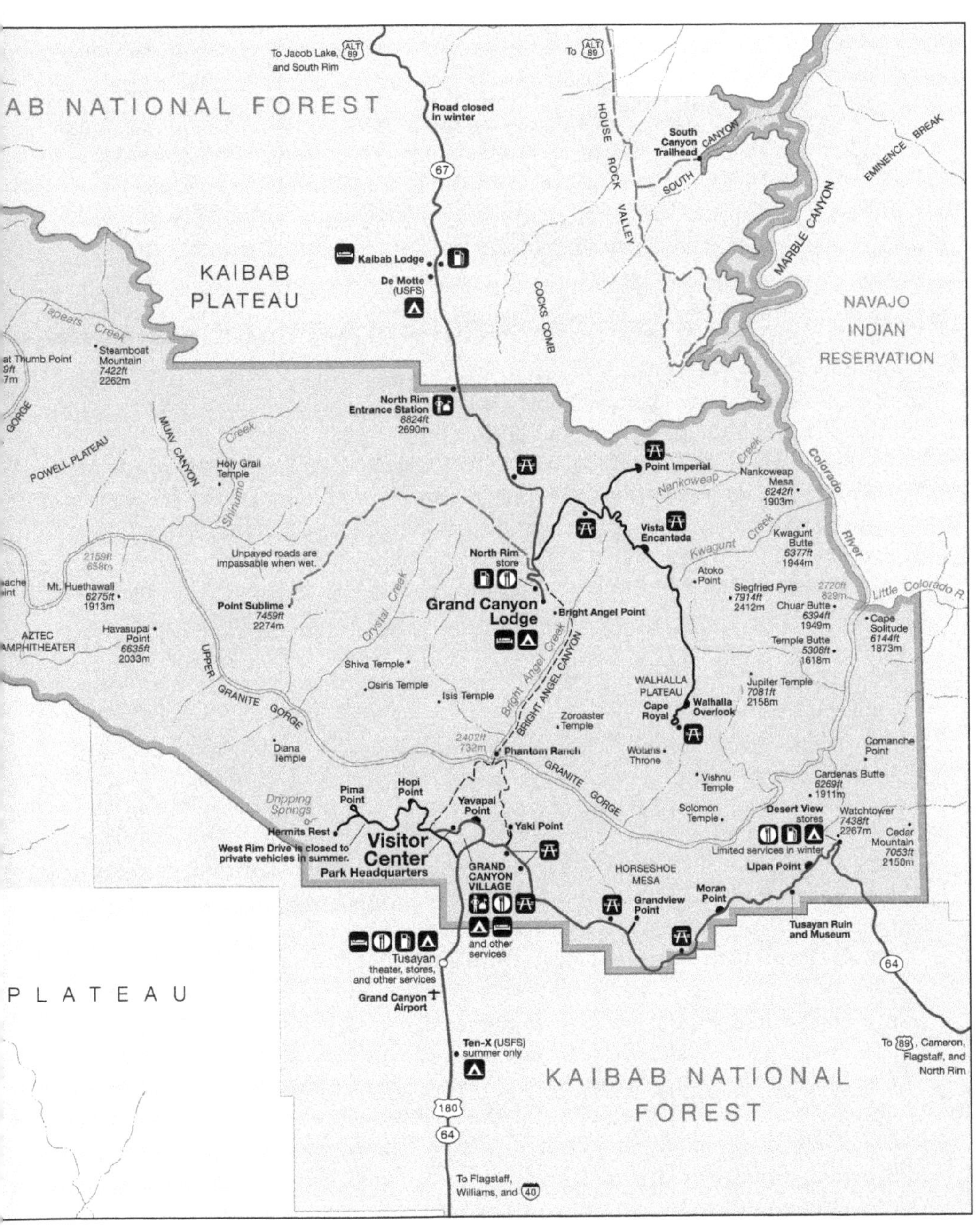

To Jacob Lake, and South Rim
To 89
KAIBAB NATIONAL FOREST
Road closed in winter
67
HOUSE ROCK VALLEY
South Canyon Trailhead
SOUTH CANYON
EMINENCE BREAK
MARBLE CANYON
KAIBAB PLATEAU
Kaibab Lodge
De Motte (USFS)
COCKS COMB
NAVAJO INDIAN RESERVATION
Tapeats Creek
Steamboat Mountain 7422ft 2262m
North Rim Entrance Station 8824ft 2690m
MUAV CANYON
POWELL PLATEAU
Holy Grail Temple
Shinumo Creek
Point Imperial
Nankoweap Creek
Nankoweap Mesa 6242ft 1903m
Colorado River
Vista Encantada
Kwagunt Creek
Kwagunt Butte 6377ft 1944m
Unpaved roads are impassable when wet.
North Rim store
Atoko Point
Siegfried Pyre 7914ft 2412m
2720ft 829m
Little Colorado R.
Mt. Huethawali 6275ft 1913m
Point Sublime 7459ft 2274m
Grand Canyon Lodge
Bright Angel Point
Chuar Butte 6394ft 1949m
Cape Solitude 6144ft 1873m
AZTEC AMPHITHEATER
Havasupai Point 6635ft 2033m
Crystal Creek
Temple Butte 5308ft 1618m
UPPER GRANITE GORGE
Shiva Temple
Osiris Temple
Isis Temple
Bright Angel Creek
BRIGHT ANGEL CANYON
WALHALLA PLATEAU
Cape Royal
Walhalla Overlook
Jupiter Temple 7081ft 2158m
Zoroaster Temple
Diana Temple
2402ft 732m
Phantom Ranch
Wotans Throne
Comanche Point
GRANITE GORGE
Vishnu Temple
Cardenas Butte 6269ft 1911m
Dripping Springs
Pima Point
Hopi Point
Yavapai Point
Solomon Temple
Desert View stores
Watchtower 7438ft 2267m
Cedar Mountain 7053ft 2150m
Hermits Rest
Visitor Center
Yaki Point
Limited services in winter
West Rim Drive is closed to private vehicles in summer.
Park Headquarters
GRAND CANYON VILLAGE
HORSESHOE MESA
Lipan Point
Grandview Point
Moran Point
Tusayan Ruin and Museum
and other services
Tusayan theater, stores, and other services
64
PLATEAU
Grand Canyon Airport
To 89, Cameron, Flagstaff, and North Rim
Ten-X (USFS) summer only
KAIBAB NATIONAL FOREST
180
64
To Flagstaff, Williams, and 40

Preface

Grand Canyon Trivia Trek represents a broad sweep through Grand Canyon National Park. It's a vehicle to enhance your Grand Canyon experience, whether away from the chasm, or on the fringe of the forested rims, or in the grasp of the Inner Canyon. This is not a trail guide, but it does provide trail descriptions. All trail miles are approximates, as reroutes become necessary to accommodate terrain breaks. Caution is advised to all who undertake even small hikes. Be prepared by consulting the National Park Service at the Backcountry Information Center for up-to-date trail and weather conditions, as well as current water availability. Check for possible highway closures that may occur due to natural obstructions, such as snow or downed trees on back area roads. All overnight hikes require a permit. Always overestimate the canyon and underestimate your ability.

Much gratitude is expressed to all in the National Park Service who provided answers to questions and concerns along the way while I documented the Grand Canyon and vicinity, including Ian Hough, Jan Balsom, Mike Quinn, Kim Besom, and Maureen Oltrogge.

Thanks to Lon Ayers, Backcountry Information Center, Grand Canyon National Park, for his willingness to hunt down bits of information and for his many years of encouragement. Those who were fortunate to hear him speak at the Mather Amphitheater during his years with the Division of Interpretation truly enriched their visit to the park by his presentation of *Summits and Side Canyons*. Today, they are enriched by the fine services he provides at the Backcountry Information Center.

Pam Cox, Phantom Ranger Station, Grand Canyon National Park, for taking crucial phone calls at the bottom of the canyon to help answer what may have seemed to be random questions, but in reality were missing historic puzzle pieces. Congratulations to Pam as she has completed a fourteen-year tour at Grand Canyon and has accepted a position at Carlsbad Caverns National Park.

Colleen Hyde, Museum Collection Department, Grand Canyon National Park, for allowing me to use her work station and for assembling the historic photographs used in this book into a working format.

Ron Clayton, Grand Canyon Mules Trail Boss, for making available to me the *Grand Canyon Livery Manual* and for "always keeping the coffee pot on." Mr. Clayton, and his impressive way of running the mule operation, has since moved from Grand Canyon National Park. He will be distinctly remembered by all who benefitted from his traditional safety talk in the Stone Corral before their muleback departure into the canyon at the head of the Bright Angel Trail.

Mira Perrizo, publisher of Johnson Books, for her insight in the preparation of this book. Also many thanks to Linda Doyle, Martin Balgach, Rebecca Finkel and all those at Big Earth Publishing that made this book possible.

IN MEMORY OF DONNA FRITTS, Tusayan Ranger District, Kaibab National Forest, who early on gave me a jumpstart in understanding the forest south of the Grand Canyon.

Introduction

My first North Rim experience at Grand Canyon National Park came courtesy of Fred Anderson in August 1976. I was thirteen years old.

Long before sunrise, Fred drove his pickup truck from Jacob Lake on Arizona State Highway 67 over the cattle guard that separates the Kaibab National Forest and Grand Canyon National Park's North Entrance Station. Traveling a ways into the park, Fred passed the turn-off for Cape Royal and headed for the small parking lot designated for the North Kaibab Trail—a fourteen-mile-long cliff-hugging route to the Colorado River. As was his habit, Fred parked the truck by turning off the ignition, letting the truck glide to a stop, and setting the parking brake. He got out of the truck in the cool air of Arizona's high country, then scouted out some good-sized rocks and chocked them under the wheels. "Keeps 'er from rollin' away on us," Fred said. "Don't want to have to pull the truck out of a ditch somewhere." Days later when we got back to the rim, called "topping out," Fred removed the rocks and put them back where he had gotten them.

Fred introduced me to "the Canyon." He is now almost eighty and still hiking. Perhaps that says as much about the influence of the Grand Canyon as it does about Fred. After my first hike with him on the South Rim's Bright Angel Trail in 1972, I gathered my first piece of Grand Canyon information. It was a modest black and white handout that described the North Rim. Hooked on the canyon, I would return year after year.

In 1980, I began an odyssey of solo backcountry hikes. By that time, I understood what the canyon required of me physically, but I only partly understood what I might encounter on the steeper, non-maintained, remote routes. For that reason, I sought out information to educate myself and to enrich my canyon undertakings. I began to study the canyon section by section. After decades of examining maps and dissecting official park documents, environmental studies, and a host of other media, I naturally became the one friends would come to when planning their own trips to the Grand Canyon. Sharing all that I had learned, I joyfully became a pro-bono travel agent.

My affection for the canyon and the knowledge gained from those years of research ultimately led to this book. And my research continues. Of the almost five million annual visitors to Grand Canyon National Park, many visit the canyon but once. Still, many return again and again to hike the Inner Canyon trails and to explore the rims of the mighty chasm. It is my hope that, with this book, you can keep a bit of the canyon with you. It is also my hope that this book will be your Fred Anderson, a strong companion initiating a profound relationship with Grand Canyon National Park.

Did You Know?

The Arizona Earthquake Information Center identifies the Grand Canyon's South Rim as the most seismically active region in the state of Arizona. **Bright Angel Fault** is an active strata terrain break. The fault passes through Grand Canyon Village and Garden Canyon below the South Rim, crosses the Colorado River, and passes through Bright Angel Canyon into the North Rim region. The fault creates the 189 feet in layer lift, as seen best in the Kaibab Limestone Formation adjacent to the Bright Angel Trail.

On line. The CCC enrollee installation of the Inner Canyon Trans-Canyon Telephone Line utilizing stunted telephone poles, ca 1935. GRCA 198

Llamas were tested as pack animals in 1985 based on their portage ability. Four animals made an attempt to traverse the canyon on the North Kaibab Trail. In the vicinity of Manzanita Creek, the llamas laid down on the trail and refused to move due to the heat of the Inner Canyon day.

The Trans-Canyon Telephone Line was completed in 1922 by the National Park Service using a single eighteen-mile long copper wire, which was strung from the South Rim to Phantom Ranch. To support the copper wire en route to Phantom Ranch, trees and rock formations were used for "telephone poles." In 1934, the Civilian Conservation Corps installed the first rim-to-rim telephone system using stunted telephone poles made of pipe and glass insulator caps. The project was completed in 1935 and maintained by Mountain Bell. Historic copper wire scraps remain along certain sections of installation.

The Esplanade is the broad expanse of the Redwall Limestone Formation that is covered by the Supai Sandstone Formation. On many wilderness trails, the Esplanade offers the shade of juniper and pinyon pine trees and is an important zone that hikers use for a campsite or to cache supplies for a return hike from the Colorado River.

The IMAX Theatre in Tusayan, Arizona, presented *Grand Canyon: The Hidden Secrets* on June 16, 1984. The film includes a portrayal of Grand Canyon's Spanish exploration and Major John Wesley Powell's 1869 expedition down the Colorado River. Expert river runners reenacted Powell and crew, and replica period boats were made for the run down the river. The boats reached the production site lashed to contracted Grand Canyon Expeditions rafts. In film production, the rafts became floating camera platforms. Forefront camera placements, such as front-of-raft and helicopter mounted camera positions, afford first-person canyon experiences.

Twin bridges. Navajo Bridge built in 1929 (left) and Navajo Bridge built in 1995 at Marble Canyon. Grand Canyon National Park's easternmost boundary. Photo by Flood Hefley

South Rim

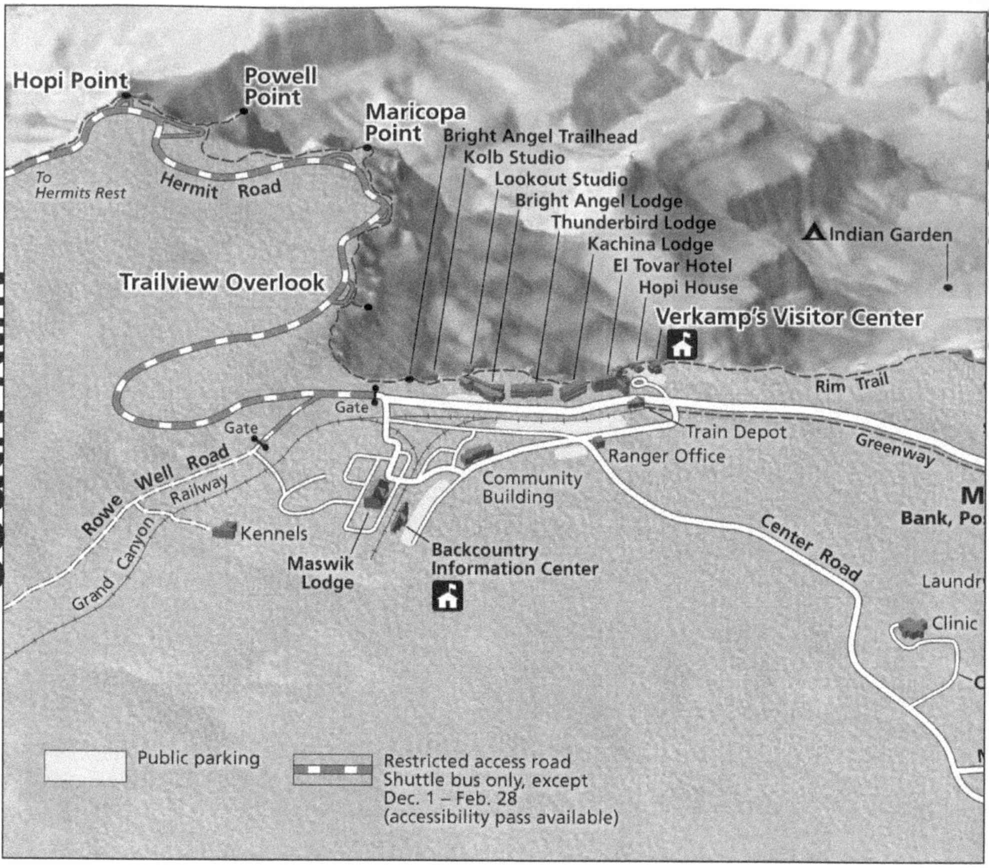

Hopi Point
Powell Point
Maricopa Point
To Hermits Rest
Hermit Road
Bright Angel Trailhead
Kolb Studio
Lookout Studio
Bright Angel Lodge
Thunderbird Lodge
Kachina Lodge
El Tovar Hotel
Hopi House
Indian Garden
Trailview Overlook
Verkamp's Visitor Center
Rim Trail
Gate
Gate
Train Depot
Ranger Office
Greenway
Rowe Well Road
Railway
Community Building
Grand Canyon
Kennels
Maswik Lodge
Backcountry Information Center
Center Road
Bank, Po
Laundry
Clinic

Public parking

Restricted access road
Shuttle bus only, except
Dec. 1 – Feb. 28
(accessibility pass available)

North Rim

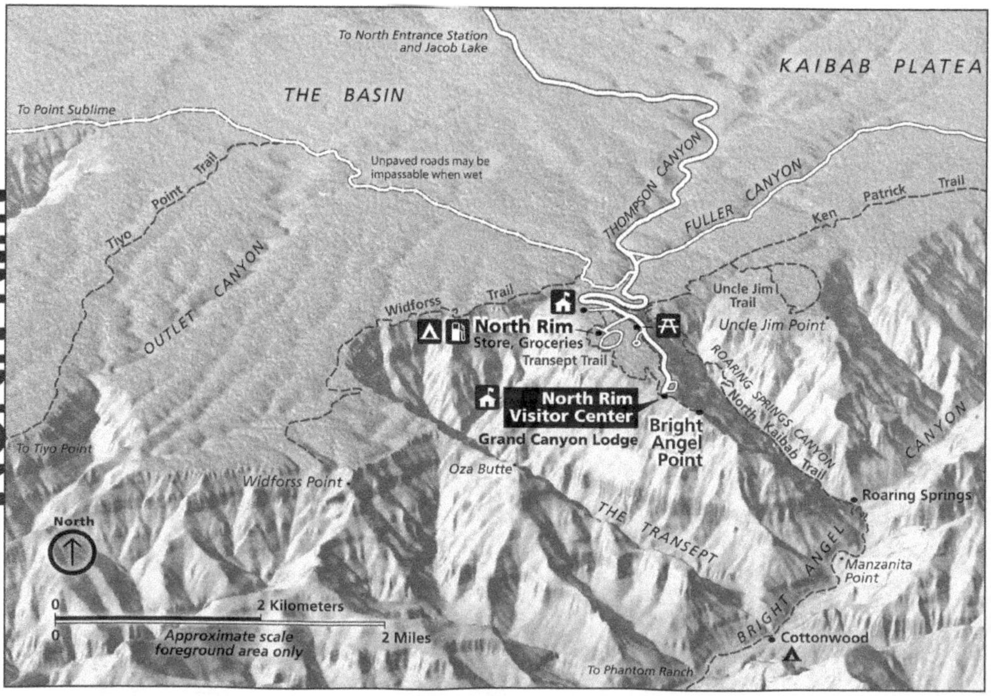

To North Entrance Station and Jacob Lake
KAIBAB PLATEA
THE BASIN
To Point Sublime
Unpaved roads may be impassable when wet
Tiyo Point Trail
THOMPSON CANYON
FULLER CANYON
Ken Patrick Trail
OUTLET CANYON
Widforss Trail
Uncle Jim Trail
North Rim
Store, Groceries
Uncle Jim Point
Transept Trail
ROARING SPRINGS CANYON
North Kaibab Trail
North Rim Visitor Center
Bright Angel Point
Grand Canyon Lodge
CANYON
To Tiyo Point
Oza Butte
Widforss Point
Roaring Springs
THE TRANSEPT
North
BRIGHT ANGEL
Manzanita Point
0 2 Kilometers
0 2 Miles
Approximate scale foreground area only
Cottonwood
To Phantom Ranch

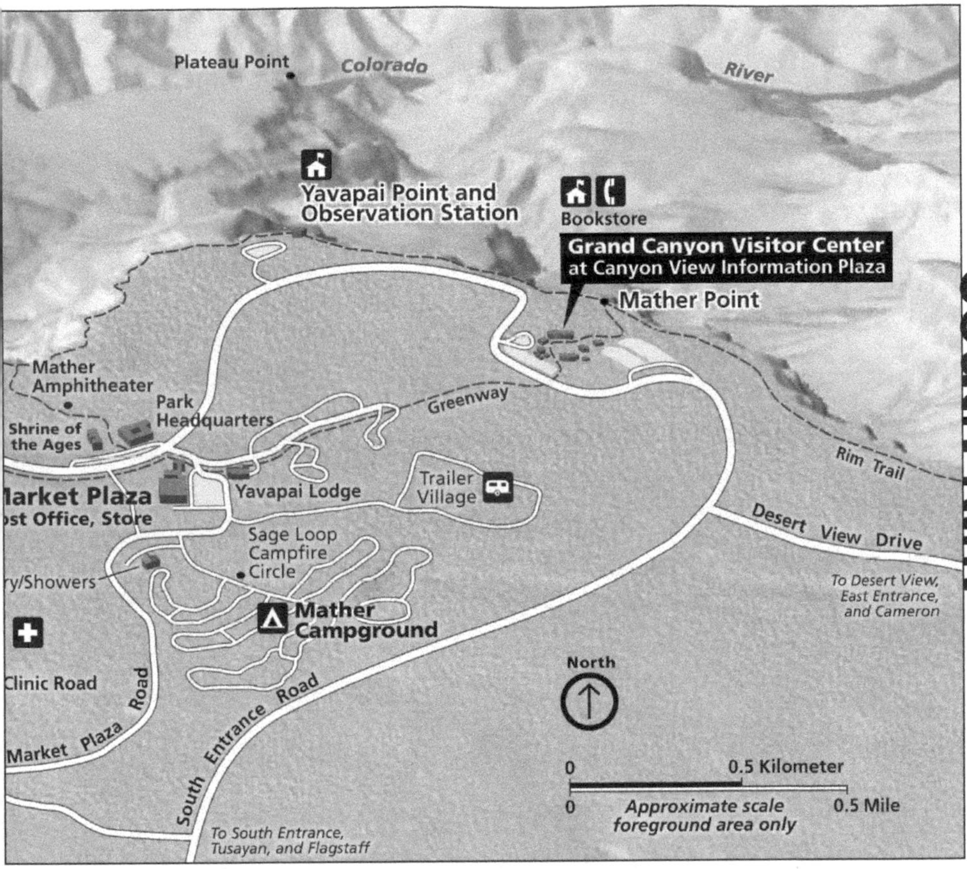

South Rim

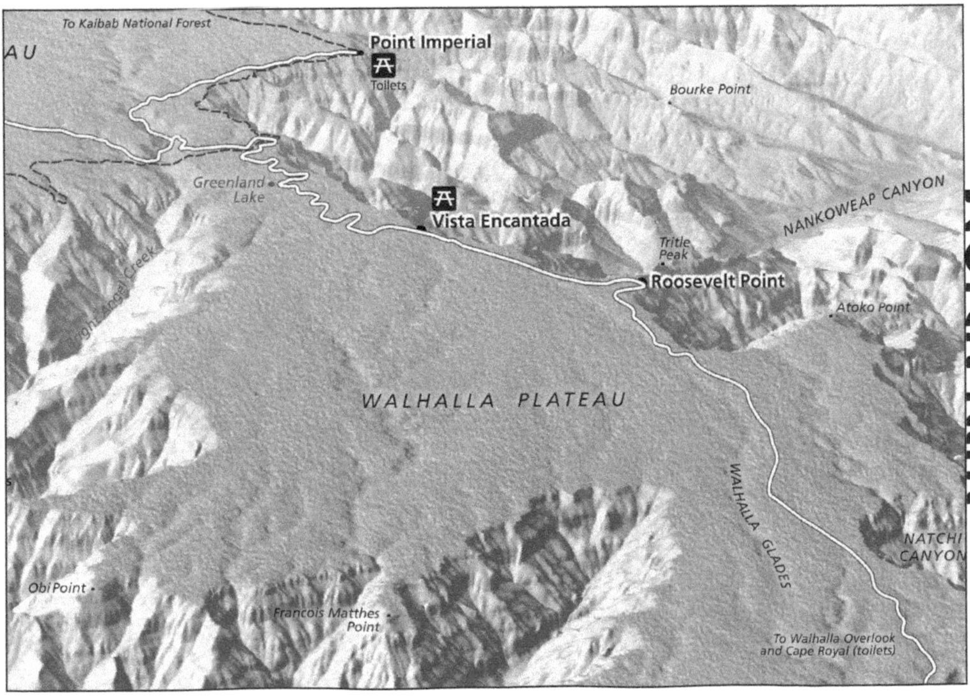

Plateau Point
Colorado
River
Yavapai Point and Observation Station
Bookstore
Grand Canyon Visitor Center
at Canyon View Information Plaza
Mather Point
Mather Amphitheater
Park Headquarters
Shrine of the Ages
Greenway
Rim Trail
Market Plaza
ost Office, Store
Yavapai Lodge
Trailer Village
Sage Loop Campfire Circle
ry/Showers
Mather Campground
Desert View Drive
To Desert View, East Entrance, and Cameron
Clinic Road
Market Plaza Road
South Entrance Road
North
0
0.5 Kilometer
0
0.5 Mile
Approximate scale foreground area only
To South Entrance, Tusayan, and Flagstaff

North Rim

To Kaibab National Forest
A U
Point Imperial
Toilets
Bourke Point
Greenland Lake
Vista Encantada
NANKOWEAP CANYON
Tritle Peak
Roosevelt Point
Atoko Point
ght Angel Creek
WALHALLA PLATEAU
WALHALLA GLADES
NATCHI CANYON
Obi Point
Francois Matthes Point
To Walhalla Overlook and Cape Royal (toilets)

Louise Hinchliffe. Grand Canyon National Parks' first research librarian, 1952. GRCA 9476

The National Park

Grand Canyon National Park is one of the Seven Natural Wonders of the World and is a World Heritage Site. Encompassing 1,904 square miles (1,218,375.54 acres) of the most rugged terrain in the United States, Grand Canyon is 277 miles long, averages ten miles wide, and is more than one mile deep between the Grand Canyon Village on the South Rim and the Grand Canyon Lodge on the North Rim. Forty-seven years after the establishment of Yellowstone National Park, Grand Canyon received its national park status. Legislative attempts were being made as early as 1882, but were delayed largely by mining lobbyists. In 1919, shortly before the park's approval, the Department of the Interior made a historic plea for action on the behalf of the Grand Canyon. On April 20, 1920, the director of the National Park Service, Stephen Mather, was master of dedication ceremonies at the South Rim's Powell Memorial, where he and Hopi Indian Chief Sacahuku and guest speakers dedicated Grand Canyon National Park. The first Superintendent from 1919 to 1920 was William H. Peters.

Grand Canyoneering: The National Park Service has a mandate to preserve resources such as their forests, along with the natural processes that sustain them, including *forest fires*. Because more than 100 years of fire suppression has interrupted the natural fire-cycle, fire itself is used as a tool by *Fire Use Management Teams* for ecosystem restoration—called a prescribed burn. When conditions are optimum, frequent low intensity fires are set and regulated. Fires that start by lightning strikes, and that burn in an undeveloped area, are monitored with resource goals in mind. The goal of the *Fire Use Strategy* at Grand Canyon National Park is to restore the natural balance found in nature by following land management practices that incorporate fire into ecosystems as a necessary natural process.

Fire extinguishers. Fire engine and truck in front of the North Rim firehouse, 1937. GRCA 9777

Grand Canyon National Park grew from its 1893 beginnings when President Benjamin Harrison proclaimed the Grand Canyon Forest Reserve. In 1906, President Theodore Roosevelt established the Grand Canyon Game Preserve. In 1908, Roosevelt reestablished the region as Grand Canyon

Vital sign. Timber and stone gateway, South Rim, 1959. GRCA 3488

National Monument. In 1917, Senator Carl Hayden introduced the Grand Canyon National Park bill. On February 26, 1919, President Woodrow Wilson signed into law Grand Canyon National Park. In 1932, President Herbert Hoover established a new Grand Canyon National Monument to the west adjoining the park. In 1969, President Lyndon Johnson established Grand Canyon National Monument to the east, also adjoining the park. In 1975, President Gerald Ford signed the bill that incorporated the 1932 and the 1969 monuments into Grand Canyon National Park.

Grand Canyon National Park key visitation years include: 1919, the year Grand Canyon became a National Park, with 44,173 visitors. The first "six-figure year" was 1923 with 108,500 visitors. The first "seven-figure year" was 1956 with 1,033,404 visitors. The years of increase by the millions include 1969 with 2,192,574, 1976 with 3,026,235, 1992 with 4,550,949 and 1997 with 5,131,011 visitors. In the years that followed, visitations remained steady, with 1999 having 4,930,153, 2004 with 4,672,911, and 2007 with 4,515,733 visitors.

Grand Canyon National Park key vehicle count years started in 1935 when the National Park Service began counting vehicles entering the park: 44,291 vehicles. The first "six-figure year" was 1946 with

Grand Canyoneering: *The River Ranger Station* was built in 1934 by the Civilian Conservation Corps adjacent to and under the general plan of The Rock House built in 1926. Also called "The Packers Cabin," the structure is located on the north bank of the Colorado River at the mouth of Bright Angel Creek on its west bank. United States Geological Survey employee Royal "Roy" Starkey resided here in performance of his duties, taking daily samples and checking the flow and temperature of the Colorado River. In the "old days," this is how the volume of river water and sediment were monitored before arriving into Lake Mead at Hoover Dam.

Rural cabin. The Rock House, Inner Canyon, 1985. GRCA 11606

Northern Arizona powder. South Entrance Station, 1931. GRCA 108

128,395 vehicles. The first "half-million year" was 1969 with 554,351. And the first "one million year" was 1991 with 1,130,840. In the years that followed, the vehicle count remained level, with 1996 having 1,370,977, 1999 with 1,423,188, and 2004 with 1,336,505.

Grand Canyon National Park was closed to visitation from November 16 to November 20 of 1995. A federal budget impasse between Congress and President William Clinton closed all National Park Service sites in that period. The National Parks and Conservation Association conducted a study that demonstrated a loss of $5.6 million in tourist related sales to Northern Arizona.

Kaibab National Forest consists of 1,555,000 acres and borders Grand Canyon National Park's North Rim (Kaibab Plateau: North Kaibab Ranger District) and South Rim (Coconino Plateau: Tusayan Ranger District). The region received its designation in 1908 by President Theodore Roosevelt, in consultation with the United States Forest Service director, Gifford Pinchot.

Wedged. Californian, Helen Hayes, collides into the South Entrance Station, 1951. GRCA 2170

Marble Canyon, formerly Marble Canyon National Monument, is the easternmost section of Grand Canyon National Park, added through the 1975 enlargement endorsement by President Gerald Ford. Major John Wesley Powell, on his 1869 Colorado River expedition, named the narrow canyon section for the polished river-level limestone. Marble Canyon extends fifty-one river miles from the Glen Canyon–Marble Canyon division at Lees Ferry, Arizona, to Saddle Mountain's Boundary Ridge.

Stephen Tyng Mather became the Assistant Secretary of the Department of the Interior and a leading advocate to form a national park service. After the formation of the National Park Service, Interior Secretary Franklin Lane appointed Mather as director. With Horace Albright, an aggressive plan was developed to enhance national park access through the railroads, such as the Union Pacific and Santa Fe. Mather established a policy of adaptability and restraint while promoting access. For example, proposals to create a lodging area at the North Rim's Cape Royal were denied, but camping was permitted. A commemorative plaque honoring Mather as the founder of the National Park Service can be found at Mather Point in Grand Canyon National Park and in Yosemite National Park in California.

The Albright Training Center, formerly the Albright Academy, serves the National Park System by providing ranger skill courses and natural resource management at the Grand Canyon since 1963. The facility was located at Yosemite National Park from 1959 to 1963, when it was known as the National Park Service Training Center. One of the many goals of the Albright Training Center is to provide skills development for new public relations employees. Horace M. Albright served as the second director of the National Park Service, following Stephen Mather, with whom he developed the National Park Service.

The Mission 66 program was a 1956 Congress-funded program that called for improved visitor facilities to be completed by 1966. Projects included the original South Rim Visitor Center–Park Headquarters, now Park Headquarters, the Mather Amphitheater (re-designated the McKee Amphitheater) for ranger-led campfire programs, and Mather Campground.

The Phantom Ranger Station is located in the canyon between Phantom Ranch and Bright Angel Campground. The station houses interpretive, law enforcement, and backcountry rangers who provide year-around services including advice, meteorology, aid and Medivac helicopter operations to hikers, mule passengers, and boaters on the Colorado River. It is also the only Inner Canyon wilderness ranger station where help may be found.

Jet Rangers. Lynn Bawden, heliport manager, and pilot Tom Caldwell (right) with Bell 206B Jet Ranger, ca 1982. GRCA 18724

Historic Camps and Campgrounds

Formal Campgrounds on Grand Canyon's South Rim include Mather (300 sites), Trailer Village (84 sites), and Desert View (50 sites). The North Rim requires fewer sites due its remoteness, which results in less visitation. North Rim Campground has 87 sites. The Inner Canyon has three formal campgrounds. They are Indian Garden on the Bright Angel Trail, and Bright Angel Campground and Cottonwood Camp on the North Kaibab Trail.

Grand Canyoneering: Desert View Campground is located near Grand Canyon National Park's East Entrance Station, approximately twenty-five miles east of Grand Canyon Village, South Rim. The campground is the optimum rim location to view sunrise. The camper is already in place as the sun progresses over the "East Rim's" Palisades of the Desert.

The back way. East Rim Drive's Desert View Entrance Station, 1935. GRCA 6543

Forest floor. Mather Campground, South Rim. GRCA D0422

Bass Camp was located on the South Rim, 15 aerial miles northwest of El Tovar Hotel at an elevation of 6,646 feet. In 1902, Grand Canyon pioneer William Wallace Bass partnered with John Waltenberg and developed

Battered by the elements. Wood-frame building at Bass Camp, South Rim, 1932. GRCA 13

Photo by Flood Hefley

Intrinsic relics. One hundred year-old coffee pots at William Bass' Shinumo Creek camp north of the Colorado River, Inner Canyon.

mining claims. When mining tapered off, the focus went to tourism. The historic camp included stagecoach service from Rowe Well and the Santa Fe's "end-of-track," near today's Maswik Lodge. The rim camp had various nicknames, including "The Yankee Girl."

Big Saddle Camp consisted of twelve cabins built by Hayden Church and family at a site 25 aerial miles northwest of the North Rim's Grand Canyon Lodge. Water was hauled from area sources such as Bee Spring, now known as Indian Hollow, 5 miles east of the historic camp. After Theodore Roosevelt's North Rim hunting excursion in 1913 illuminated the region, the camp accommodated the rising number of sport hunters.

Bright Angel Camp was the original name given to the South Rim's Bright Angel Hotel, the predecessor of Bright Angel Lodge. The Bright Angel Camp and Hotel were built by stagecoach entrepreneur James Thurber, and were managed by Grand Canyon pioneer Martin Buggeln until 1906. Thurber's stage line from Flagstaff, Arizona, reached this South Rim region in 1896. The wood-framed and

Inner Canyon shelter. Commonly referred to as "Camp 818," CCC Company 818's camp (officially NP-3-A, Phantom Ranch) on the west bank of Bright Angel Creek south of Phantom Ranch, ca 1935. GRCA 3775

canvas-covered tent cabins of the hotel remained intact into the 1930s. They were gradually replaced as the timber cabins of today went into service with the Mary Jane Colter designed Bright Angel Lodge.

Bright Angel Campground is located in the canyon, 7 aerial miles southwest of the North Rim's Grand Canyon Lodge, at an elevation of 2,500 feet. The campground serves hikers of the North and South Kaibab and Bright Angel and River Trails. The 1930s Civilian Conservation Corps Company 818's camp NP-3-A, Phantom Ranch, commonly called "Camp 818" was located in this area and served as base camp for Inner Canyon trail building. Overnight stays in Bright Angel Campground require a National Park Service overnight permit.

Grand Canyoneering: Inclusive of the Colorado River and its threshold shores, the Main Corridor refers to the centered Inner Canyon region framed within the North Rim's Grand Canyon Lodge and Bright Angel Canyon, the South Rim's Grand Canyon Village and Garden Creek Canyon, and the area of the Tonto Trail between the Bright Angel and South Kaibab Trails.

Cottonwood Camp, locally called Cottonwood Basin, is located approximately halfway down the North Kaibab Trail at an elevation of 4,000 feet. The area is noted for the density of Fremont cottonwood trees that flourish along Bright Angel Creek.

Hermit Camp, at an elevation of 2,960 feet, was a historic Inner Canyon lodge that included wood-framed, canvas-covered, tent cabins. The area was developed in 1910 and located 4 aerial miles west of the South Rim's El Tovar Hotel. The camp included a dining hall that was staffed by a Fred Harvey Company chef. In the 1920s, the camp was serviced by an aerial tram that was stationed on the South Rim at Pima Point. The tram was removed by the National Park Service after the camp's use was discontinued in 1930 due to the growing development of tourist facilities in and on the canyon rims of the Main Corridor. To remove the entire camp itself, on November 9, 1936, the National Park Service razed the buildings by ordering a prescribed structure burn.

Nestled in time. Hermit Camp, 1914. GRCA 5121

Over land route. Hermit Camp supply tram stationed at Pima Point, 1936. GRCA 786

Bunk houses. Ralph Cameron's Inner Canyon cabins and stone lodging at Indian Garden, ca 1932. GRCA 8

Recycled stones. Ben Beamer's Inner Canyon "cabin" located at the confluence of the Colorado and the Little Colorado Rivers—and at the end of an extreme twenty-mile-long backcountry route network. Built in 1891, Beamer utilized this overhang and dismantled a nearby ruin for its masonry. GRCA 5173a

Grand Canyoneering: Remote Grand Canyon trailheads can be accessed by a combination of state highways, light-duty paved roads, U.S. Forest Service and National Park Service dirt roads, and the more challenging *jeep trails*. After leaving a formal road, driving routes may become obscure due to a lack of signs, fallen trees, and washouts. These routes often terminate at unimproved sites and are best reached by a high-clearance 4-wheel drive vehicle. Extra travel items that will aid in an unforeseen extended stay in the wilderness include emergency water and food. Outdoor equipment may include lantern, cold and wet weather gear, and sleeping bag. Tools may include a compact floor jack, which provides stability and "reach" to a vehicle that is on uneven ground. Vehicle replacement parts should include battery, headlights, and two spare tires. Once outside a developed area, help may be several days away.

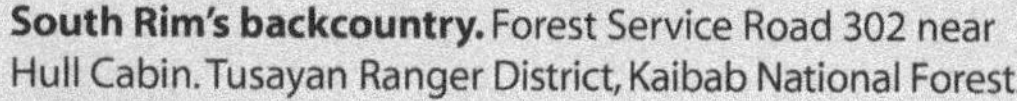

South Rim's backcountry. Forest Service Road 302 near Hull Cabin. Tusayan Ranger District, Kaibab National Forest.

Ranger Station:

Why does the National Park Service engage two thermometers on the information kiosk at the northern entrance to the Inner Canyon's Bright Angel Campground? One thermometer is located in direct sunlight and, just as significant because the difference could be a matter of life and death, another thermometer is located in the shade. The shaded thermometer, surrounded by blinders that keep it out of direct sunlight, measures the temperature a hiker would experience when ducking under the limited shade of a boulder, cliff, tree, or shrub.

Ranger Station:

Desert View Campground is twenty-five miles away from the services of Grand Canyon Village. What makes it worth going so far out? Located on the eastern outskirts of Desert View, on the South Rim, the campground provides immediate rim access to view the sunrise.

Indian Garden and Camp is located in the canyon 1.5 aerial miles north of the South Rim's El Tovar Hotel in Garden Canyon, at an elevation of 3,870 feet. The area was cultivated by Native Americans who grew melons, squash, corn, and beans. Indian Garden is the Inner Canyon's primary travel hub for hikers and mule passengers, which makes it the busiest Inner Canyon stop below the rim. River runners starting a "half-trip" also visit this site as they pass through to meet a river company at the Colorado River. River runners also exit the canyon after their half-trip. The site is also the location of the Trans-Canyon Water Line pumping station, which converts the gravity fed water from the North Rim's Roaring Springs to pumped, sometimes termed "pushed," water. From Indian Garden, the water continues to the South Rim's discretely placed fourteen million gallon holding tanks.

Inner Canyon Trails, Routes, and Trail Sections

Trails, over time, have acquired individual names for certain **trail sections.** Some of the names have long since fallen into disuse such as the Bright Angel Trail's Cape Horn, which was bypassed by a man-made tunnel. As a National Park Service maintained trail may become unstable through their continual use by mule trains, a trail such as the Bright Angel Trail continually encounters a maintenance schedule and sometimes phases of reconstruction.

Grand Canyoneering: Northern Arizona University math professor Harvey Butchart (1907–2002) logged more than 12,000 canyon miles, documented new routes, and wrote the most consulted Grand Canyon backcountry book, *Grand Canyon Treks* (1976). His first hike was in 1945, when he hiked the South Kaibab, River, and Bright Angel Trails. Butchart's backpack and boots reside in the Grand Canyon National Park Museum Collection Department.

The Arizona Trail System, organized by Dale Shewalter in 1985, is the 750-mile-long route that crosses Arizona from the northern state line at Utah to the southern border at Mexico. To cross the state and Grand Canyon, the trail must utilize the North and South Kaibab Trails, and the Kaibab Suspension Bridge, to pass over the Colorado River.

The North and South Bass Trails were developed by Grand Canyon pioneer William Wallace Bass. The trails were improved Cohonina and Havasupai Indian routes, and by 1906 Bass had installed a trans-canyon trail system that serviced his mining claims and tourist interests. The trails were linked by his cableway that was upgraded in 1908 to include a suspended cage.

The North Bass trailhead is located approximately 15 aerial miles northwest of the North Rim's Grand Canyon Lodge at an elevation of 7,517 feet, and is a 14-mile-long route from the rim at Swamp Point to the Colorado River. The trail descends to the Muav Saddle and the historic Muav Saddle Cabin. The route turns sharply south as it continues below Powell Plateau into White Canyon. Below White Canyon, the route proceeds to the

Photo by Flood Hefley

Vigorous water colors. Cliff-shaded pools and chutes at perennial Shinumo Creek, North Bass Trail.

North Bass Trail, and South Bass Trail end at its junction with the Tonto Trail, Inner Canyon, USGS *Grand Canyon National Park and Vicinity*

strong flow of Shinumo Creek. The trail then passes through historic Bass Camp and on to the Colorado River via an overland route that bypasses a waterfall near river level.

The South Bass trailhead is located approximately 16 aerial miles northwest of the South Rim's El Tovar Hotel and is a 7-mile-long route, which leaves the South Rim at Bass Point, at an elevation of 6,646 feet, and leads to the Colorado River. The trail runs down to the Esplanade, and then continues down along the Redwall Limestone Formation. Once below the Redwall, the trail continues to the Tonto Trail and the Colorado River.

> **Ranger Station:**
> **Why is the North Kaibab Trail in Bright Angel Canyon? And why is Bright Angel Trail in Garden Creek Canyon?** During the late 1800s and early 1900s, the route from the Colorado River to the North Rim was the north section of the contiguous Bright Angel Trail System. (The presently unmaintained trail through upper Bright Angel Canyon to the east of Roaring Springs Canyon is designated the Old Bright Angel Trail. The trail is sometimes referred to as the North Angel Trail or the Old Kaibab Trail.) In 1924, the National Park Service changed the designation from Bright Angel Trail to Kaibab Trail while planning to complete a new upper section through Roaring Springs Canyon. Bright Angel Trail through the South Rim's Garden Creek Canyon was formerly the Cameron Trail, named after owner Ralph Cameron.

Photo by Flood Hefley

Backcountry camping. Once away from the Main Corridor, camping is at large along the 100 rouge miles of the Tonto Trail. Here, like much of Grand Canyon National Park, the reality of the canyon is bold—there is little to no contact with shade, water, or other hikers.

The Beamer Trail is named for Ben Beamer, who lived in a stone cabin by the Little Colorado River. The Beamer Cabin was built in 1891 under an overhang that was used for the roof, and the stones of an adjacent Indian ruin became the cabin's walls. This route is located between the Little Colorado River and the sand dunes at the end of Seth Tanner's Tanner Trail in the eastern section of the canyon.

The Boucher Trail is a 10-mile-long route that branches off from the Hermit Trail and travels to the Colorado River. Beginning in 1902, the trail supported the mining claims of Louis Boucher. The trail can also be accessed from the Dripping Springs Trail and the Waldron Trail, the trailheads of which are located on the rim of the Hermit Basin. The route traverses scree slopes that abut side canyon rims.

The Bright Angel Trail is 7.8 miles long from the trailhead at the Kolb Studio to the Colorado River. It is an additional 1.7 miles from the Colorado River to

Bright Angel Campground via the River Trail, the cliff-side route between the Bright Angel Trail and the South Kaibab Trail, and the Silver Suspension Bridge. Phantom Ranch is an additional .2 miles along the North Kaibab Trail. The first forms of the historic, world famous Bright Angel Trail

Grand Canyoneering: Switchbacks are a meandering trail technique by which trails double back above and below themselves to make possible a consistent ascent and descent of an eroded or collapsed cliff—a *terrain break*. The break is held by *dry laid stone*—essentially a brick wall made without mortar that is backfilled to level out a trail. The switchback terrace is stabilized by check steps formed with evenly placed rock and timber native to the Colorado Plateau, such as Utah juniper. Switchbacks are stabilized through *cribbing*, a method that utilizes courses of timber and *water bars*—countersunk logs in the trail that divert rain water and snow melt.

Conspicuous descent. Jacob's Ladder in the Redwall Formation, Bright Angel Trail. GRCA T408

Above: **Tucked away.** Mile-and-a-Half Resthouse with historic thatched roof (since replaced with shingles), Bright Angel Trail, ca 1935. GRCA 900
Left: **On the edge.** Three Mile Resthouse at the top of the Redwall Formation cliffs, Bright Angel Trail, ca 1936. GRCA 901
Below: **At trail's end.** The River Resthouse at the Colorado River and Pipe Creek, Bright Angel Trail, ca 1936. GRCA 889

were pathways established by Native Americans. The first improvements were made by John Hance, and modernization began circa 1897 when claim holder Ralph Cameron improved the route to support his mining interests. By 1903, the route was extended to the river. The trail at this time was known as the Cameron Trail until the National Park Service acquired the trail in 1928 and made further improvements by 1938. The Bright Angel Trail is a former toll trail where, at the trailhead, $1.00 was collected for each person and livestock animal passing by. Today, in the trail section above Indian Garden, there are two resthouses that were built in the 1930s by the Civilian Conservation Corps. Each has drinking water in the summer. In the winter, the water is turned off to keep the pipes from freezing. The first resthouse is 1.5 miles from the trailhead and the second is 3 miles. Hence the names Mile-and-a-Half and Three Mile Resthouse. At the Colorado River is the River Resthouse.

Trail tractor. Mule-drawn "ditcher" invented by Jack Watson, 1965. GRCA 4792h

Bright Angel Trail Sections

Cape Horn is a reconstructed turn of the upper Bright Angel Trail named for Wollaston Island's Cape Horn in Chile. The trail section was circumvented by a manmade tunnel that was blasted through a fin of rock, like the tunnel nearer to the South Rim, in 1912. This particular passageway could be termed the "Cape Horn Tunnel."

Cinch Up Point is located .25 mile from the trailhead. Before continuing farther into the canyon, mule wranglers (also called mule skinners) stop their mule trains and check the tightness of each passenger's (also called dudes) saddle.

On the trailing edge. Adam Limbach and Grand Canyon pioneer Emery Kolb (rear) ride the brink of the Bright Angel Trail's Cape Horn, ca 1906. GRCA 15828

Two-Mile Corner serves as the reference point for travelers that are between the resthouses in the upper trail section. Approximately 200 yards above the turn and facing upwards toward the South Rim, pictographs can be seen on the east face of a house-sized boulder. It is thought that the pictographs were made by the Havasupai during their occupation of this side canyon.

Rock art. Pictographs on house-size boulder above Two-Mile Corner, Bright Angel Trail, 1978. GRCA 10993

The Devil's Corkscrew is the trail section that descends 1,200 feet through the Vishnu Schist Formation along steep elongated switchbacks. The name of the section may be confirmed by any backpacker who is ascending the trail during the middle of a summer day. The original section, built in 1899 by Ralph Cameron's brother, Niles, was steeper and resulted in mule train passengers dismounting and leading their mounts to the base of the cliff.

The Jacob's Ladder switchback was built on a man-made "break" in the Redwall Limestone Formation below the Three-Mile Resthouse. Western author George Wharton James described the switchback as a "series of sheer steps chiseled" into the Redwall cliff.

The Thunder River and Bill Hall Trails access the Thunder River, Tapeats Creek, Deer Creek, and Deer Creek Falls. At its Indian Hollow trailhead, elevation 6,240 feet, the Thunder River Trail is located 29 aerial miles northwest of the North Rim's Grand Canyon

High velocity. Deer Creek Falls plunges 125 feet out of Deer Creek Narrows at Colorado River mile 136.3. GRCA RIV0008

Lodge. The route was pioneered between 1876 and the 1880 arrival of geologist Clarence Dutton. It was improved in 1926 by patrons of Big Saddle Camp. The alternate route is the Bill Hall Trail. This trailhead is located 27 aerial miles northwest of the North Rim's Grand Canyon Lodge at Monument Point, elevation 7,206 feet. This route bypasses the Thunder River Trail at its Indian Hollow trailhead and cuts five miles off the trip to the Surprise Valley junction at an elevation of 3,600 feet. The tradeoff is 966 feet of elevation gain. The Bill Hall Trail (sometimes referred to as a "horse trail") is named for ranger Ward "Bill" Hall, who was killed in an ambulance accident. The on-site plaque at Monument Point reads: *Dedicated to the memory of park ranger Ward "Bill" Hall who gave his life in the line of duty for the safety of park visitors at the North Rim of Grand Canyon National Park on July 16, 1979.* The **Deer Creek Trail** travels west from Surprise Valley and descends the Deer Creek Narrows to the Colorado River and Deer Creek Falls.

Grand Canyoneering: "Pack-it-in, Pack-it-out" is the National Park Service's Inner Canyon cargo policy. If you carried it into the canyon or away from developed rim areas such as Grand Canyon Village, South Rim and Grand Canyon Lodge, North Rim, you are required to carry it back out. There is no garbage service in these wilderness areas.

The Cable Trail provided access from the Bright Angel Trail, then Cameron Trail, at Indian Garden to a trolley site in the vicinity of today's Kaibab Suspension Bridge. The route crossed the Tonto Plateau, the broad expanse located 1,200 feet above the Colorado River, from which the Cable Trail then descended through the Inner Canyon in the vicinity of today's South Kaibab Trail. The route name was prompted by David Dexter Rust's cable-suspended aerial trolley over the Colorado River. Today the route exists as a section of the Tonto Trail.

The Cape Royal Trail is the .5-mile long trail that travels on top of the relatively narrow Kaibab Limestone Formation peninsula. The paved path travels between the mature cliff rose and juniper and pinyon pine trees of the North Rim's Cape Royal. The path ends along and behind the guarded rim of the canyon with the spectacular views of Vishnu Temple and Wotans Throne. As a side note,

Grand Canyoneering: The three-mile long backcountry *Royal Arch Route* is accessed after traveling the South Bass Trail and the Apache Point Trail west of Grand Canyon Village. Another approach is via the South Bass Trail to the Tonto Trail West to Garnet Canyon. At the mouth of Garnet Canyon, the Colorado River–level trail continues as the 2.5-mile long *Elves Chasm Route*. These routes should only be attempted by hikers who are highly experienced Grand Canyon backpackers. The former route requires a twenty-foot rappel and the equipment recommendations of fifty feet of UIAA rated rope, leather gloves, thirty feet of webbing, harness, rappel ring, and carabiners, along with knowledge and skill with their use. Garnet Canyon, where there is a stream of bitter tasting water, is located nineteen aerial miles northwest of Grand Canyon Village.

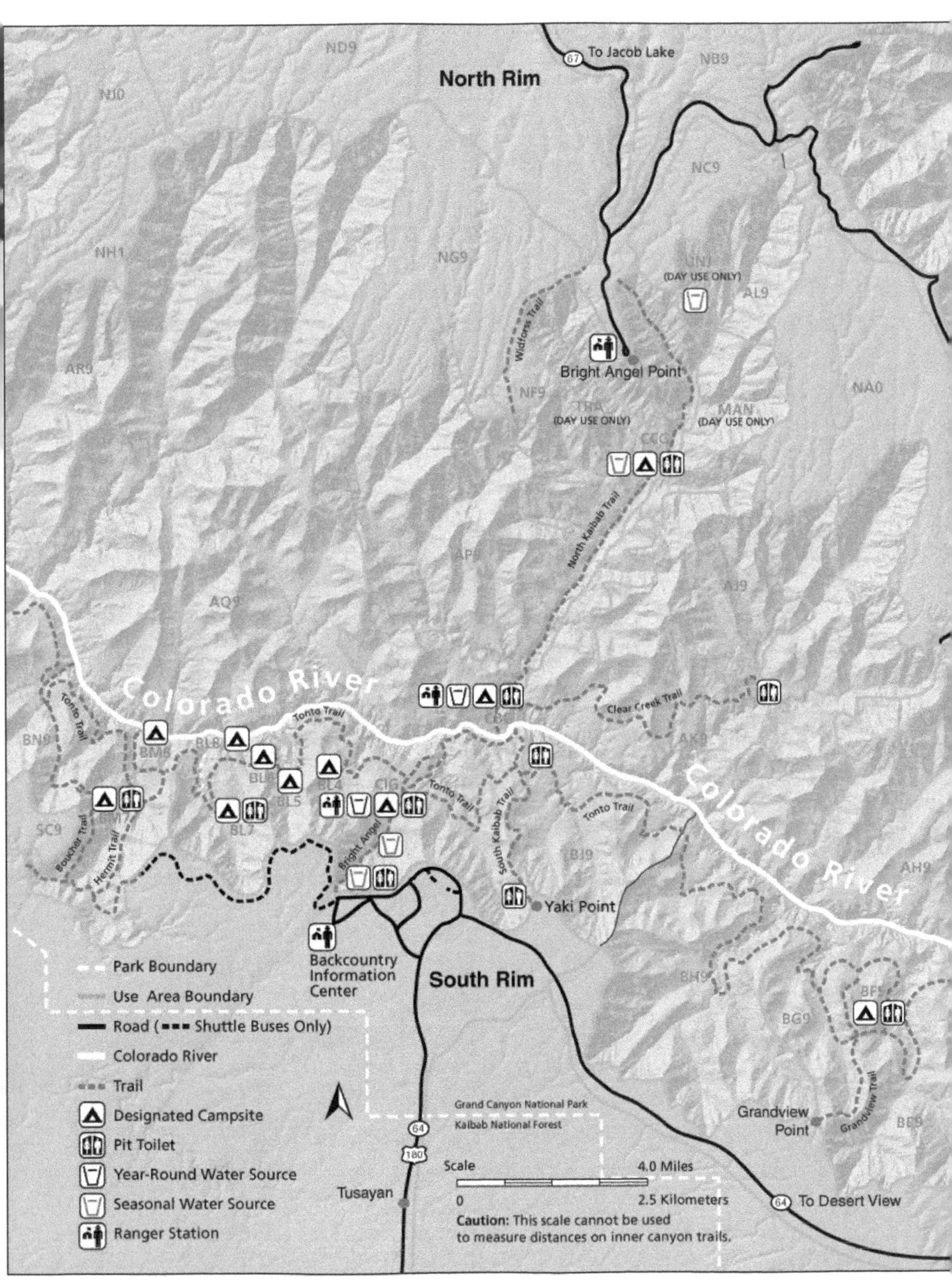

Grand Canyon Main Corridor Backcountry map.

Wotans is "missing" its apostrophe 's' because cartographers often omit such punctuation because it can become confused with other notations such as the symbol for "feet" or become "lost" within a map's contour lines.

The Grand View Trail was built by Peter D. Berry 10 aerial miles southeast of the South Rim's El Tovar Hotel. It is 3 rugged miles long from the rim to the end of the trail on Horseshoe Mesa. The trail was reconstructed in 1902 to accommodate guests of the Grand View Hotel. In its original form, the trail was precarious. Some trail sections were constructed using logs chained to the upper cliff faces.

The New Hance Trail is an 8-mile long route from the South Rim. The trailhead is located along the Desert View–East Rim Drive 1 mile southeast of Moran Point. "New" in this case means not the original. John Hance relocated his trail through Red Canyon after the original trail through Hance Canyon was washed out in 1895. The alternate name for the New Hance Trail is the Red Canyon Route, and the original route through Hance Canyon is commonly called the Old Trail.

Hermit Trail & Sections

The Hermit Trail is the 8.5-mile-long backcountry route from its trailhead on the South Rim, 8 aerial miles west of the South Rim's El Tovar Hotel, to the Colorado River. Formerly referred to as the El Tovar Trail, the route intercepts the Tonto Trail in the area below the Cathedral Stairs trail section. The route accesses the perennial Hermit Creek and the class 8 Hermit Rapid at river mile 95.

Grand Canyoneering: When hiking the canyon, you will be descending from the rim with a full backpack. By the end of the hiking day, the physical results from fighting the pull of gravity are inflamed muscles, sensitive tendons, and sore toes, which cause an awkward gait known locally as *The Kaibab Shuffle.*

The Stone Shelter at Santa Maria Spring is located 2 miles below the trailhead. The shelter was built in 1913 as part of the development of Hermit Camp.

Breezy Point was named by the Kolb Brothers, Ellsworth and Emery, and is located at an elevation of 3,200 feet. This trail section overlooks Hermit Creek Canyon.

Bunker Hill Monument is named for prospector and trail builder Fred Bunker. The "monument" is a section of the trail in the Redwall Limestone Formation. Bunker also played a key role in the development of the Tanner Trail near Desert View.

The Cathedral Stairs descends the Hermit Trail down to the Tonto Plateau and Trail through fossilized seashells and sea lily stems.

The Hopi Trail is a historic trade route that originates from the Hopi settlement of Oraibi, Arizona, approximately 60 aerial miles southeast of the Grand Canyon. The route travels west and ends at Moqui Trail Canyon, then continues five trail miles to Havasu Canyon and the village of Supai of the Havasupai Indians.

The Horsethief Trail is a combination of the Tanner Trail from the South Rim and the Nankoweap Trail from the North Rim. "Horsethief," as one word, is the local term applied to this territorial rustler's route of the 1880s and 1890s. In those years, rustlers drove livestock from Utah to sell in Arizona and returned to Utah over the same route with livestock stolen in Arizona. Occasionally, with altered brands, the same livestock would be sold back to the ranches from which they were rustled. Rustlers considered altering brands an art. In the days of the telegraph, some could change the old brand with a piece of red-hot telegraph wire. Along the route, at one or more rock outcrops, rustlers would position themselves to ambush a posse. These sites became known as a *robber's roost.*

The Kaibab Trail System is the 20.8-mile-long rim-to-rim route that is divided at the Kaibab Suspension Bridge on the Colorado River. From the South Rim, the

On belay. Grand Canyon National Park trail crew repairing a section of the South Kaibab Trail. GRCA

Sky light. The north end of Suspension Bridge Tunnel, South Kaibab Trail tail. GRCA D1258

descent begins adjacent to Yaki Point and is the South Kaibab Trail. From the North Rim, the descent is through Roaring Springs Canyon and lower Bright Angel Canyon. This is the North Kaibab Trail. The trail north of the Colorado River began as animal pathways through the entire Bright Angel Canyon. These paths were enhanced by the use of ancient Indian peoples. In 1902, François Matthes of the United States Geological Survey substantially improved the route, locating the trailhead in the vicinity of Neal Spring, northeast of present-day Grand Canyon Lodge. In 1907, Utah tourism promoter David Dexter Rust further developed the route, then known as the Rust Trail. In 1924, the National Park Service changed the name to the "Kaibab Trail" while planning the re-route out of upper Bright Angel Canyon and through the entire Roaring Springs Canyon and the lower Bright Angel Canyon. The South Kaibab Trail did not yet exist at the time. It would be a freshly constructed trail that would meet the historic route coming from the north to access historic Phantom Ranch. By design and necessity, the South Kaibab's steep trail was built along the tops of many Inner Canyon ridge lines. Because it is based on ridge lines, the trail provides

Grand Canyoneering: The 90-foot-long tunnel at the end of the South Kaibab Trail was blasted out of the region's Vishnu Schist Formation on the south bank of the Colorado River. The tunnel's northern threshold is located at the foot of the Kaibab Suspension Bridge, also called "The Black Bridge." The South Kaibab Trail is founded on ridge lines making it extremely exposed to the elements. This makes the tunnel important to summer travel because Bright Angel Campground and Phantom Ranch are still a good distance away along the North Kaibab Trail, and the tunnel is the only section of the South Kaibab Trail that provides continuous shade.

Eye level. Hiker on the South Kaibab Trail faces Brahma (left) and Zoroaster (right) Temples. GRCA D7270

incredible views, not only north into the canyon, but also east and west into the canyon's interior. Construction of the trail system began in 1924 and was completed in 1928 with the assembly of the Kaibab Suspension Bridge—locally called the "Black Bridge." Prior to the North Kaibab's formal opening by the National Park Service, 100 wet crossings of Bright Angel Creek were required to reach the Colorado River. The first form of bridge over the creek was boards set on rocks, which were replaced after the passing of high water. In later years, the plank bridges were chained to the rocks to keep them from washing away in flood waters. This would be particularly true of the bridges located in The Box, Bright Angel Canyon's slot canyon, or "narrows," section. Ultimately, the crossings were reduced to four in The Box and three more bridges—the Ribbon Falls Bridge, the Roaring Springs Trestle, and the dramatic Redwall Bridge—located in the upper trail sections. The National Park Service constructed the South Kaibab Trail in large part to circumvent the toll that was first imposed by Ralph Cameron, and then Coconino County, on the Bright Angel Trail. Coincidentally, the county waived the toll fee after the completion of the new trail in exchange for a road traveling between Williams, Arizona, and the Grand Canyon.

Cliff hanger. North Kaibab Trail in Roaring Springs Canyon.

Grand Canyoneering: *Cairns,* from the Gaelic term for "heap," are rocks stacked in specific numbers to help define a hiking route. In Grand Canyon travel, however, these landmarks are commonly stacked "to be seen" above ridges and brush for hikers ascending out of the backcountry. ***Route finding ability*** is the skill of determining the common or best minimum-impact path over difficult terrain.

Rees B. Griffiths was a National Park Service trail foreman who was killed by a rockslide triggered by a dynamite blast. He is buried in Grand Canyon alongside the North Kaibab Trail, near the mouth of Bright Angel Creek. His epitaph reads: *Died Feb. 6, 1922, in the Grand Canyon that he loved so well as a result of injuries received near this spot while in the performance of his duty in the building of the Kaibab Trail.* Griffiths is one of six people formally interred outside the boundaries of the Grand Canyon Pioneers Cemetery in Grand Canyon National Park. Also are John and Merribeth Riffey at the North Rim's Tuweep area and, site undisclosed, the Brant's (and their dog Razzle Dazzle) who managed the Grand Canyon Depot. One could say that there was a sixth, as pioneer William Wallace Bass was cremated and had his ashes distributed over Holy Grail Temple—also called Bass Tomb.

Rock-steady mules. "Dudes" approaching journey's end on The Chimney of the South Kaibab Trail. GRCA T431

South Kaibab Trail Sections

The Chimney is located 3 aerial miles east of the South Rim's El Tovar Hotel and is named for the uppermost "semi-stovepipe" switchbacks descending from the trailhead.

> **Grand Canyoneering:** Cape Solitude is accessible under the conditions of "non-mechanized travel," as defined by the National Park Service. Providing for the wilderness, non-vehicular travel to this remote locale is sometimes carried out on mule or by horseback. By permission from the Diné (Navajo) to travel their land to the National Park's southeast boundary, the water-less Cape Solitude Trail makes the final approach to the rim.

Ooh Aah Point is located 2 aerial miles northeast of the South Rim's El Tovar Hotel at an elevation of 6,350 feet. The hairpin turn allows the first dramatic below-the-rim east-to-west Inner Canyon views after departure from the trailhead in the Yaki Point region.

Cedar Ridge is located 1.5 miles from the trailhead and is a hiker and mule trail destination. At an elevation of 6,067 feet, Cedar Ridge resides 2,200 feet distant from the massive O'Neill Butte and is a mere 3 feet higher in elevation.

Natural history. Fossil fern exhibit at Cedar Ridge, South Kaibab Trail. GRCA 9374A

Mormon Flats, at an elevation of 5,250 feet, is named for the growth of the plant, Mormon Tea, and the relatively level walk unique to this area.

Skeleton Point is located approximately 2 trail miles below the South Rim, at the top of the Redwall Limestone Formation, at an elevation of 5,250 feet. Circa 1925, a failure to tether a string of pack mules with slipknots forced an entire mule train to accompany the lead mule when it veered off of the trail and fell over the area's sheer cliffs. For several years, the mules' skeletons remained at the base of the promontory.

The Red and Whites are one of the trail's major switchback series. The name is suggested by the man-made geologic break in the Redwall Limestone Formation, which creates an alternating pattern of gray (the actual internal color of the Redwall Limestone) and red (the external color of the formation, a coating of iron oxide washed down from the canyon layers above).

Breeze way. Windy Ridge, South Kaibab Trail. GRCA D2604

Grand Canyoneering: Officially, the Grand View Trail is a 3-mile-long route from the South Rim to its end on Horseshoe Mesa. Three secondary trails lead off the mesa and connect with the Tonto Trail East. From what is known as *Mesa Junction*, a westerly route travels 1.4 miles to Cottonwood Creek. Also from the junction, another 1.4-mile-long trail known as The Mesa Route travels the slender west arm of Horseshoe Mesa, and then descends .8 mile as a steep scramble to the Tonto Trail. Thirdly, a .9-mile route travels eastward from a point where the mesa "attaches" to the main canyon wall below Grand View Point. This route accesses the main workings of Pete Berry's **Last Chance Mine**. Farther along, the route reaches Miner's Spring, also called Page Spring, for John H. Page of the Canyon Copper Company. Ultimately, this easterly route junctions with the Tonto Trail and Hance Creek.

The Tipoff is located approximately 5 trail miles below the South Rim at an elevation of 4,000 feet. Indicating "something confidential is going to happen," the Tipoff in this case indicates where the trail discreetly descends the Tonto Plateau located 1,200 feet above the Colorado River. This is the region where the historic Cable Trail, now lost to erosion and the routing of the South Kaibab Trail, crested the Granite Gorge rim and descended to the river and the Rust Aerial Trolley.

Poison Point is a tight 'S' turn switchback configuration in the trail at an elevation of 3,675 feet.

The Train Wreck is located at an elevation of 3,875 feet and is descriptive of the "derailed train" look of the terrain in the area just up-trail from Panorama Point.

Panorama Point provides a northerly view up into Bright Angel Canyon and Phantom Ranch from an elevation of 3,600 feet, 1,200 feet above the Colorado River. The overlook also provides east-to-west views of the Inner Gorge and Boat Beach—the river runners' staging area for trips that are continuing through the remaining river system.

Photo by Flood Hefley

Lofty ledge. Panorama Point above the Colorado River at the confluence of Bright Angel Creek, South Kaibab Trail. Notice the Silver Suspension Bridge crossing the Colorado at river mile 88.

North Kaibab Trail Sections

The Coconino Overlook is located at an elevation of 6,750 feet, one-eighth of a mile down the trail. The wide-open view is the interior of Bright Angel Canyon.

Supai Tunnel, at an elevation of 7,000 feet, is a man-made, 32-foot-long tunnel that was blasted out of the Supai Sandstone Formation during construction of the North Kaibab Trail. Two trail miles below the trailhead, the tunnel circumvents the upper cliffs of Roaring Springs Canyon.

The Redwall Bridge circumvents the trail section that washed out in 1966 below Supai Tunnel. Trail remnants are still visible on the west slope of Roaring Springs Canyon.

Photos by Flood Hefley

Above: **A sleepy hollow.** Lower end of Supai Tunnel, North Kaibab Trail.
Right: **On the Redwall Bridge.** Traversing Roaring Springs Canyon, North Kaibab Trail.

The Needle is a Redwall Limestone Formation pinnacle at an elevation of 6,200 feet.

The Needle's Eye was at an elevation of 6,200 feet. The Inner Canyon man-made tunnel feature was a Redwall Limestone Formation section of the trail that yielded to erosion.

Photo by Flood Hefley

Bypassing a landslide. The Redwall Bridge, North Kaibab Trail.

The Nankoweap Trail is a 14-mile-long route that leaves the North Rim at an elevation of 8,800 feet at Saddle Mountain. This route to the Colorado River is based on ancient Indian travels. The trail was improved in 1882 by geologist Charles Doolittle Walcott, under the directorship of Major John Wesley Powell, to give the United States Geological Survey access to the northeastern canyon region. The trail descends into this remote region of the national park and ties into the perennial Nankoweap Creek and the Colorado River at the class four–rated Nankoweap Rapid. This area contains abundant evidence of occupation by the Ancestral Puebloan. The Nankoweap Ruin is a classic example, perched 500 feet above river level at an elevation of 3,300 feet, under an overhang in the Nankoweap Mesa (photo pg. 105).

Grand Canyoneering: In 1936, Daniel Lorain Hogan constructed the Grand Canyon Inn on the property of the Lost Orphan Mine. Operated initially by the Golden Crown Mining Company, the inn was west of Maricopa Point adjacent to the historic Hermit Rim Road. The original name of the inn was the Grand Canyon Trading Post. When Will Rogers Jr. acquired the property in 1949, the inn became known as Rogers' Place and operated until 1966. Daniel Hogan also worked the Hermit Basin area 8 miles west of Grand Canyon Village. Hogan and Henry Ward built the **Waldron Trail,** which runs from a north facing bay of the South Rim at Horsethief Tank for two miles into the canyon where it junctions with the Hermit Trail. No one knows for certain why Hogan named his trail "Waldron." Introduced here, the trail's name may originate from Hogan's travel path from Syracuse, New York, through Waldron, Arkansas, of the Ouachita Mountains. The region is noted for pine timber, resembling the look of Hermit Basin. Hogan, an orphan, may have searched the town of Waldron for forebears where the Hogan name fills the census reports.

The Tanner Trail was developed in the 1880s by Arizona Territory pioneer Seth Tanner and prospector Franklin French, who improved "a way down into the canyon." The route was used originally by the Hopi and the Navajo, and it is possible that prior to the use by these Native American groups the region was traveled by the Ancestral Puebloans. In the 1880s, it was called the Tanner-French Trail, and the historic trailhead was located in Tanner Canyon. The Tanner Trail descends the South Rim from its trailhead at Lipan Point at an elevation of 7,380 feet. Near Desert View, the trail loses 4,740 feet of elevation over its 9-mile course. The trail aggressively descends approximately 2 trail miles from the rim to the Esplanade, typically a broad expanse of the Redwall Limestone Formation capped by Supai Sandstone Formation, found here in the eastern section of the canyon in the form of "saddles" where, usually at night, high winds charge over these ridge lines. After crossing the Esplanade for approximately 3 miles, the route descends the Redwall. While on this section of the trail, the Indian Watchtower is small, but often in plain view. The route progresses along the lower ridge that separates Cardenas Creek from Tanner Canyon. The trail continues on the Cardenas Butte talus slope to Tanner Creek and the Colorado River at an area locally called Furnace Flats. This is the easternmost established rim-to-river trail that also became known as the Horsethief Trail (see Horsethief Trail).

Furnace Flats is an open and shadeless sandbar expanse located at the end of the Tanner Trail—the mouth of Tanner Canyon. Due to the Grand Canyon's east-to-west alignment, the area is long exposed to the sun. Summer daytime temperatures can reach 130 degrees.

The Lava Falls Trail, also called The Lava Route, is located in the Toroweap area in the Tuweep region, 62 aerial miles west of the South Rim's Grand Canyon Village. The trailhead is located at the base of a dormant volcano called Vulcan's Throne. This is the steepest and shortest officially named rim-to-river route in the canyon. The trail descends 2,800 feet from the North Rim to the Colorado River in 1.5 miles. By comparison, the Bright Angel Trail descends 2,900 feet from the South Rim to Indian Garden in 4.5 miles. On the Lava Trail, at approximately the halfway point, the trail section is locally called "The Treadmill." In this section, the trail gives way under foot and causes a hiker to slide backward with the feeling of not making a rapid headway. The section is located between two cliffs on pumice rubble, which rests at the steepest angle of repose—the steepest angle in which sediment will lie without cascading down. Former North Rim ranger, John Riffey, has often humorously said, "But sometimes it doesn't repose." The end of the Lava Falls Trail resides at class ten rapid Lava Falls.

Grand Canyoneering: The Boundary Ridge formation includes Saddle Mountain at an elevation of 8,424 feet. Sieber Point, elevation 6,880 feet, and Marion Point, elevation 5,600 feet, are extensions of Boundary Ridge. Based on ancient Native American travels, the 14-mile long Nankoweap Trail starts at Saddle Mountain. It was developed by geologist Charles Doolittle Walcott. This trail was improved to gain access to the eastern Grand Canyon in order to support geological research under the United States Geological Survey's director, Major John Wesley Powell.

The Rim Trail is a 12-mile-long South Rim nature trail, also called the Greenway. The Rim Trail is paved from the Yavapai Observation Station to Trail Overlook, and continues unpaved west to Hermits Rest. Recent additions include the

Dedicated ranger. Grand Canyon National Park Ranger Ken Patrick (1933–1973) at the head of the Tanner Trail after search and rescue mission. Patrick transferred to Point Reyes National Seashore, California, where, tragically, he was murdered by deer poachers. **The Ken Patrick Trail** extends ten heavily forested North Rim miles from the North Kaibab Trail, at an elevation of 8,241 feet, to Point Imperial, at an elevation of 8,803 feet. GRCA 3034

section from Yavapai Point to Mather Point. At the time of this publication, further enhancements are planned to make the trail system 73 miles long and to include sections on the North Rim.

The River Trail provides a 1.7-mile access between the base of the Bright Angel and South Kaibab Trails. The Civilian Conservation Corps built the trail between 1933 and 1936 by blasting the Inner Canyon's Vishnu Schist cliffs to "ledge-out" a route bed. Injuries were probable, so an ambulatory mule was trained by Marvin Gandy, who ironically was beset with appendicitis and had to be transported out of the canyon on the mule he trained. The crew earned $30 per month in addition to food, clothing, and shelter. Company 818 quartered in an area that is now Bright Angel Campground. The camp, officially NP-3-A, Phantom Ranch, but commonly called "Camp 818" included 50 tent cabins, a cook tent, and a recreation hall (photo pg. 6). At the north end of Bright Angel Campground, to grant access to Phantom Ranch, a wooden footbridge was located 100 feet downstream from the permanent steel bridge of today. In one section, the trail passes through a sand dune environment.

Intrepid route. CCC enrollees building the River Trail high above the Colorado River. GRCA 242

The Tonto Trail is named for the Tonto Apache Indians and is located south of the river on the Tonto Plateau. The trail terrain alternates between the Granite Gorge, 1,200 feet above the Colorado River, and open stretches that follow brinks of side canyons. The approximately 95-mile-long wilderness route extends west from the end of the Hance Trail at Red Canyon to Garnet Canyon. The east-to-west traveling Tonto Trail helps to make "loop hikes" possible by connecting with other trails that travel south and north. Hikers seldom travel the entire route that is divided east and west of Indian Garden—defined as Tonto East and Tonto West. At the eastern end, the trail continues as the Esplanade Route to the end of the Tanner Trail. The route continues yet farther east to the Little Colorado River as the Beamer Trail. At the western end, the trail continues west of Garnet Canyon as the Elves Chasm Route, which travels to the river level grotto called Elves Chasm.

Skeleton Point and O'Neill Butte on the horizon. The Tonto Trail between Indian Garden and the South Kaibab Trail. GRCA D3143

The Tuckup Trail consists of many different sections with varying points of entry. Tuckup is slang for Tucket of the Tucket Mining Corporation. The primary trailhead is east of Toroweap Overlook where the route accesses Cove Canyon. The route continues east and can access Big Point, Stairway, Willow, Fern Glen, Tuckup, and 150-Mile Canyons. The route can also access Kanab Creek. The route is ambiguous. In defining the Tuckup Trail, it has been humorously said, "It would pose no real problems ... as long as you don't mind being lost at least half the time, and off-course the other half."

The Widforss Trail, named for artist Gunnar Widforss, is a 5-mile-long North Rim route that follows the heavily forested north and west rim contour of The Transept. The trail ends at an elevation of 7,882 feet at Widforss Point, 2 aerial miles southwest of the North Rim's Grand Canyon Lodge.

Photo by Flood Hefley

Trailhead. Near Moran Point, the Hance Trail descends the South Rim into the backcountry.

Ranger Station:

How long does it take to hike out of the canyon? Every trail is different with regard to grade, condition, and the amount of maintenance it receives. The rule of thumb is: Double your time. It will take twice as long to travel out of the canyon as it took to get into the canyon. If it took an hour to travel to the Mile-and-a-Half Resthouse on the Bright Angel Trail, count on it taking at least two hours to make it back to the South Rim.

Renowned Grand Canyon hiker Harvey Butchart humorously described the ascent of the South Kaibab Trail this way, "Getting back to the South Rim will separate the men from the boys. Starting from the river, the boys arrive back at the trailhead in a little more than four hours while the men need an extra hour."

Ranger Station:

Why should everyone stay on the trail? The Grand Canyon is a demanding environment for travel, a place where those who shortcut established trails unwittingly damage the fragile terrain. Cross-cutting switchbacks damages the vegetation between the switchback, loosens and topples boulders toward hikers below, and promotes unnatural erosion. In hindsight, travelers most often discover that the established trail would have been much easier to travel, anyway. "Minimum Impact" is the program designed to reduce the damaging effects of travel in the park. On routes, in particular, when the path is not prevalent, choose a sandstone (slickrock) surface.

Tuweep & Toroweap Regions

Toroweap is located 62 aerial miles west of the North Rim's Grand Canyon Lodge. Officially named Grand Canyon National Park, Tuweep Subdistrict, this region is one of the most remote locales in the contiguous United States, where access is only attempted by those adequately prepared to cope with the possible problems associated with remote desert travel. After the canyon was formed, more than sixty volcanic cones changed the topography. An often-overlooked biotic community exists seasonally in the red slick-rock pockets. "Fairy shrimp" and tiny frogs emerge from the muddy bottom of the recesses when rainwater fills the pools for a sufficient amount of time. From 1942 to 1980, this region was patrolled solely by ranger John Riffey.

Grand Canyoneering: On a summer expedition in 1880, United States Geological Survey geologist Clarence Dutton, who named many of the Inner Canyon formations, wrote of the Toroweap Overlook in the Grand Canyon district of Tuweep, *We approach the lower end of Toroweap. The scenery here becomes colossal. Its magnitude is by no means its most impressive feature, but the precision of the forms... It is hard to realize that this is the work of the blind forces of nature.*

The Arizona Strip is a 397,300-acre corridor between the Grand Canyon's North Rim and the state of Utah. One of the true values of this land mass is that it creates a preservation buffer between civilization and the Grand Canyon. From the high deserts of the Toroweap Valley to the pine forests on Mount Trumbull, the land supports increasingly rare regional wildlife, such as the desert tortoise of the Strip's Grand Wash Cliffs Wilderness and the black bear of the Saddle Mountain Wilderness. The Vermilion Cliffs region of Marble Canyon is the California condor wilderness release site.

Photo by Flood Hefley

Above: **Lonely outpost.** Tuweep Ranger Station, ca 1935. GRCA 215
Left: **The Sunshine Route.** Main road into Tuweep at Arizona State Highway 389.

High country. Toroweap Overlook, North Rim. GRCA

Sharlott Hall served as the Arizona Territory's first historian in 1909. With writings and lectures, Hall challenged Utah's early 1900s Arizona Strip–North Rim region annexation attempts. From July 23 to December 5, 1911, by team and wagon, Sharlott Hall traveled with guide Allen Boyle from Flagstaff, Arizona, to Lees Ferry, Arizona. The duo then headed west across the Kaibab Plateau, and, by a circuitous route, documented the unknown and disputed region. Hall alerted Arizona's political establishment to the value and advantages of the North Rim and the need to retain the land. On gaining statehood in 1912, Arizona succeeded in holding the land.

Toroweap Overlook is located 62 aerial miles west of the North Rim's Grand Canyon Lodge at an elevation of 4,552 feet. Toroweap Overlook should not be confused with Toroweap Point, which is recessed from the North Rim. Toroweap Overlook provides an unobstructed vertical view of the Colorado River 2,877 feet below.

Toroweap Point, located 62 aerial miles west of the North Rim's Grand Canyon Lodge at an elevation of 6,203 feet, is recessed from the general contour of the North Rim. Almost 2,000 feet higher in elevation, Toroweap Point should not be confused with Toroweap Overlook.

Vulcan's Anvil, located in the volcanic Toroweap region, sits in the Colorado River at river mile 178.5. Also called **Vulcan's Forge,** the formation is a 70-foot high lava neck protruding out of the middle of the river and is the remains of a volcanic vent.

Vulcan's Throne is located in the volcanic Toroweap Valley just west of the Toroweap Overlook. Vulcan's Throne is a 500-foot high cinder cone remnant of an extinct, sometimes referred to as dormant, volcano that is positioned on the very brink of the North Rim.

John Hauert Riffey (1911–1980) was the sole National Park Service ranger at the North Rim's remote Tuweep Subdistrict. In this region that is simply called *Toroweap*, Riffey served a 36-year term, from 1942 to 1980

Lone ranger. Tuweep Ranger John Riffey, 1980. GRCA 5871

Grand Canyoneering: Ranger John Riffey stationed his airplanes at a dirt airstrip that was constructed by Bud Kent. The rough dirt airstrip, nicknamed the *Tuweep International Airport,* is located in Toroweap Valley near the Tuweep Ranger Station. From his airplanes that he named *Pogo,* Riffey kept an eye out for forest fires, lost hikers, and deer hunters. Many times, those approaching by car or truck would travel off-course, or someone would attempt to drive through a muddy gully and get stuck at the bottom. When Riffey would show up with his truck equipped with a winch, the motorist would always inquire how he knew they were stuck there. He would also be alert to cattle stranded in a *cattle guard*—a gate-less metal grate countersunk into the road within a fence line to retain area livestock.

A little house on the prairie. Kent Ranch in the Tuweep Valley. The Kents: Bud, Mattie, and son Amos, ca 1939. GRCA 394

with a two-year absence for military duty in World War II. Ranger Riffey successively owned and patrolled in two Piper Cubs that he named *Pogo*. He kept the planes on a rough-hewn airstrip under a ramada-hangar, which he dubbed Tuweep International Airport. His first plane had a small range. Riffey eventually sold this plane and purchased a second plane, which had the longer range of 600 miles. Preflight inspection of the airplanes included removing a box of mouse poison from the wings, to which John would remark, "Pogo is only made out of lightweight materials." Sometimes, Riffey would hear mice scurrying about. During one of the plane's pre-maintenance inspections, three rodent nests were discarded from the wings. So, naturally, Riffey was concerned the mice would gnaw through something crucial. The planes were dependable. One time, however, Riffey was flying 3,000 feet over the canyon, near Toroweap Overlook, when a spark plug became loose in the plane's engine, which caused the plane to stall for a moment. Riffey said, "It was OK ... my hair had already turned gray." Riffey felt that his major contribution to society was "keeping Tuweep like it is." *Toroweap* is a compound of the Paiute words *toro*, meaning "dry" or "barren" and *weap*, meaning "canyon."

Ranger Station:

What is the significance of Vulcan's Anvil? Also called Vulcan's Forge, Vulcan's Anvil is the 70 foot high "lava neck," or duct, protruding out of the middle of the Colorado River below Toroweap Overlook. To river runners, this is the defining landmark, or warning, that the ten-plus-rated Lava Falls Rapid is at hand.

Ranger Station:

What is the Arizona Strip? Toroweap is a regional unit of the Arizona Strip located between the North Rim and the state of Utah. The Arizona Strip provides a natural conservation and preservation buffer by way of its naturally rugged and remote terrain.

Inner Canyon Formations:
Buttes, Temples, Points, Mesas, Plateaus, and Exotic Designations

The Alligator, descriptive of the Inner Canyon formation, is located 1.5 aerial miles northwest of the South Rim's El Tovar Hotel at an elevation of 5,600 feet, below Hopi and Mohave Points. The promontory was named by Grand Canyon pioneer Emery Kolb.

Shadow symphony. Desert View to Angels Gate (mid-ground). GRCA D3647

Angels Gate is a geological formation located 8 aerial miles southeast of the North Rim's Grand Canyon Lodge. Angels Gate is thought by the Diné (Navajo), Hopi, and the Paiute Indians to be the site where *Those Above*, who created the Grand Canyon, would one day return to Earth. Because the east and west profile of the formation resembles the Charles M. Schultz *Peanuts* character Snoopy reclining on his dog house, the local name for Angels Gate is "Snoopy Rock."

Grand Canyoneering: The Toroweap rim area, called *The Esplanade*, is formed of Supai Sandstone and Redwall Limestone Formation cliff faces. This is a high desert region with the heat and thunderstorms of summer, and with the cold and snow of winter. Toroweap Valley is a chaparral ecosystem containing pinyon pine and Utah juniper, sagebrush and woody plants, bunchgrass and Mormon tea. At an elevation of 4,552 feet, Toroweap is best reached using a high-clearance 4-wheel drive vehicle. There are three access routes. Drive 1 is *The Sunshine Route*, a 59-mile-long road from Fredonia, Arizona. Drive 2 is *The Clayhole Route*, a 55-mile-long road from Colorado City, Arizona. Drive 3 is *The Main Street Route*, a 90-mile-long road from St. George, Utah. All of these routes may become impassable during rain or snow. The National Park Service manages the terrain for its primitive values, so improvements are uncommon and services are nonexistent. There is no water, food, or fuel. Travelers should carry two spare tires, towrope, snow chains (for snow or mud), basic auto repair items, and tools.

Wild west. Weather-beaten trestle on the Sunshine Route, Tuweep Valley, North Rim.

Photo by Flood Hefley

Sunset palette. The Battleship Iowa (foreground) and Isis Temple (background), South Rim. GRCA D2147

The Battleship geological formation is located adjacent to the Bright Angel Trail 0.5 aerial miles north of the South Rim's El Tovar Hotel, at an elevation of 5,855 feet. The complete name of the butte is *The Battleship Iowa*. In 2003, the westerly cliffs were monitored for California condor nesting activity.

Beale Point, elevation 6,560 feet, is located 23 aerial miles northwest of the North Rim's Grand Canyon Lodge. The formation is named for Arizona explorer and surveyor Edward F. Beale, who also experimented with the camel as a United States War Department pack animal. The subject camels were imported from Egypt and Turkey.

Grand Canyoneering: John Muir, the founder of the Sierra Club, pleaded for the creation of Grand Canyon National Park. He said of the Grand Canyon that it was, "Where the prudent keep silence [in] nature's capital city."

Bedivere Point is located 11 aerial miles northwest of the North Rim's Grand Canyon Lodge at an elevation of 7,600 feet and is named for the famous knight of the Round Table, Sir Bedivere.

Blue Moon Bench is located 22 aerial miles northeast of the South Rim's El Tovar Hotel at an elevation of 6,000 feet. The formation forms the East Rim of the canyon in the vicinity of the Indian Watchtower. It is said that it is named so because it is visited infrequently—"Once in a blue moon."

Boundary Ridge is located 12 aerial miles northeast of the North Rim's Grand Canyon Lodge at an elevation of 8,639 feet. Boundary Ridge is the former National Park boundary. As signed into law by President Gerald Ford, the boundary is now located adjacent to the Navajo Bridges of 1929 and 1995, farther east near Lees Ferry at the head of Marble Canyon.

Boysag Point is located 38 aerial miles northwest of the North Rim's Grand Canyon Lodge at an elevation of 5,590 feet. Boysag Point's narrow margin between itself and the rim was accessed by planks laid out from the rim to the point. *Boysag* is the Paiute Indian word for "bridge."

Bradley Point is located 7 aerial miles south of the North Rim's Grand Canyon Lodge at an elevation of 5,200 feet. The formation is named for Major John Wesley Powell's 1869 expedition crew member, George Young Bradley. Bradley rescued Major Powell, who was slipping to his death from an Inner Canyon ledge, by extending his longjohns to the Major for lack of rope.

Grand Canyoneering: The Grand Scenic Divide is located 16 aerial miles northwest of the South Rim's El Tovar Hotel at an elevation of 5,600 feet. The divide is a 1.5-mile-long ridge line formation that separates Bass and Serpentine Canyons and serves as a scenic demarcation. Prevalent east of the divide are the butte, temple, and tower formations. Prevalent west of the divide are the terrace, plateau, and amphitheater formations.

Brady Peak is located 6 aerial miles northeast of the North Rim's Grand Canyon Lodge at an elevation of 8,107 feet. The peak is named for Arizona Territory legislature member, Peter R. Brady. Renowned hiker Harvey Butchart first noted that "Brady Hole" is a twenty-foot diameter hollow in the crest of a Redwall Limestone Formation alcove on the east side of the peak.

Bridger's Knoll is located 27 aerial miles northwest of the North Rim's Grand Canyon Lodge at an elevation of 6,603 feet. The formation is named for fur trapper Jim Bridger. Grand Canyon fur trappers did not explain in detail where they encountered fur-bearing animals—just as a prospector did not reveal the location of his claim.

Bright Angel Point is located immediately southeast of the North Rim's Grand Canyon Lodge at an elevation of 8,145 feet. The peninsula formation resembles a ship's prow jutting out into Bright Angel Canyon.

Vertical topography. From Bright Angel Point, North Rim. Left to right: Deva and Brahma Temples, and Hattan Butte. GRCA T008

Cape Final is located 9 aerial miles southeast of the North Rim's Grand Canyon Lodge at an elevation of 7,916 feet and provides views of Juno and Jupiter Temples. Because of the limited access by a 1.7-mile-long trail, the formation retains a place of great solitude, while in the midst of a semi-developed area. The overlook provides a mile-after-mile view of The Painted Desert, which is across and east of the Grand Canyon.

Cape Royal is located 8 aerial miles southeast of the North Rim's Grand Canyon Lodge at an elevation of 7,865 feet. Cape Royal is one of the few formal North Rim vantage points that have a view of the Colorado River.

Cape Solitude is located in the remote East Rim backcountry 21 aerial miles southeast of the South Rim's El Tovar Hotel at an elevation of 6,146 feet. Cape Solitude's alternate name is "Cape Desolation," as described by Grand Canyon pioneer Ellsworth Kolb. Cape Solitude provides a view of the confluence of the Colorado and Little Colorado Rivers, 3,446 feet below.

Cardenas Butte, named for Spanish explorer Captain Don Garcia Lopez de Cardenas, is located 17 aerial miles east of the South Rim's El Tovar Hotel.

Cedar Mountain is located 20 aerial miles east of the South Rim's El Tovar Hotel. East of Desert View, at an elevation of 7,054 feet, the top of the mesa-like mountain is 384 feet lower than Desert View. From the top of the Indian Watchtower, the difference is 454 feet. The trees of Cedar Mountain were misnamed by the Spanish explorers of the 1500s and are Utah juniper. The mountain is a remnant of the regionally eroded Moenkopi Sandstone Formation, but is a strata that is common to the north of Grand Canyon in Utah.

Grand Canyoneering: On May 6, 1903, President Theodore Roosevelt addressed the people on behalf of the Grand Canyon from the porch of the Bright Angel Hotel. A celebrated portion of the speech:

Leave it as it is. Man cannot improve on it... The ages have been at work on it and man can only mar it. What you can do is leave it for your children, and your children's children and all who come after you, as one of the great sights which every American, if he can travel at all, should see.

Bully! John Hance with President Theodore Roosevelt (on horse), ca 1911. GRCA 1573

Cheops Pyramid is a butte formation located 6 aerial miles southwest of the North Rim's Grand Canyon Lodge at an elevation of 5,350 feet. The site is named for the pyramid at Gizeh, near Cairo, which entombed the Egyptian Pharaoh, Cheops. Backpacker Harvey Butchart notes that Cheops Window is a fifteen-foot by fifteen-foot broken rock outcropping at the top of the northern buttress.

Chikapanagi Mesa and Point are located 33 aerial miles northwest of the South Rim's El Tovar Hotel and are named for Havasupai tribal member Chikapanagi, whose name means "bat." In the opinion of the Havasupai, Chikapanagi had a "bat-like" face.

Coronado Butte, located 11 aerial miles southeast of the South Rim's El Tovar Hotel at an elevation of 7,108 feet, is named for Spanish explorer Francisco Vasquez de Coronado, who in the year 1540 commanded the first organized exploration of today's Southwestern United States. In his efforts, Coronado dispatched an entourage that ultimately discovered the Grand Canyon at the South Rim in the vicinity of Desert View.

The Desert Facade, located 23 aerial miles northeast of the South Rim's El Tovar Hotel, is the eastern ridge section of Marble Canyon, where the elevation ranges from 5,760 feet to 6,061 feet.

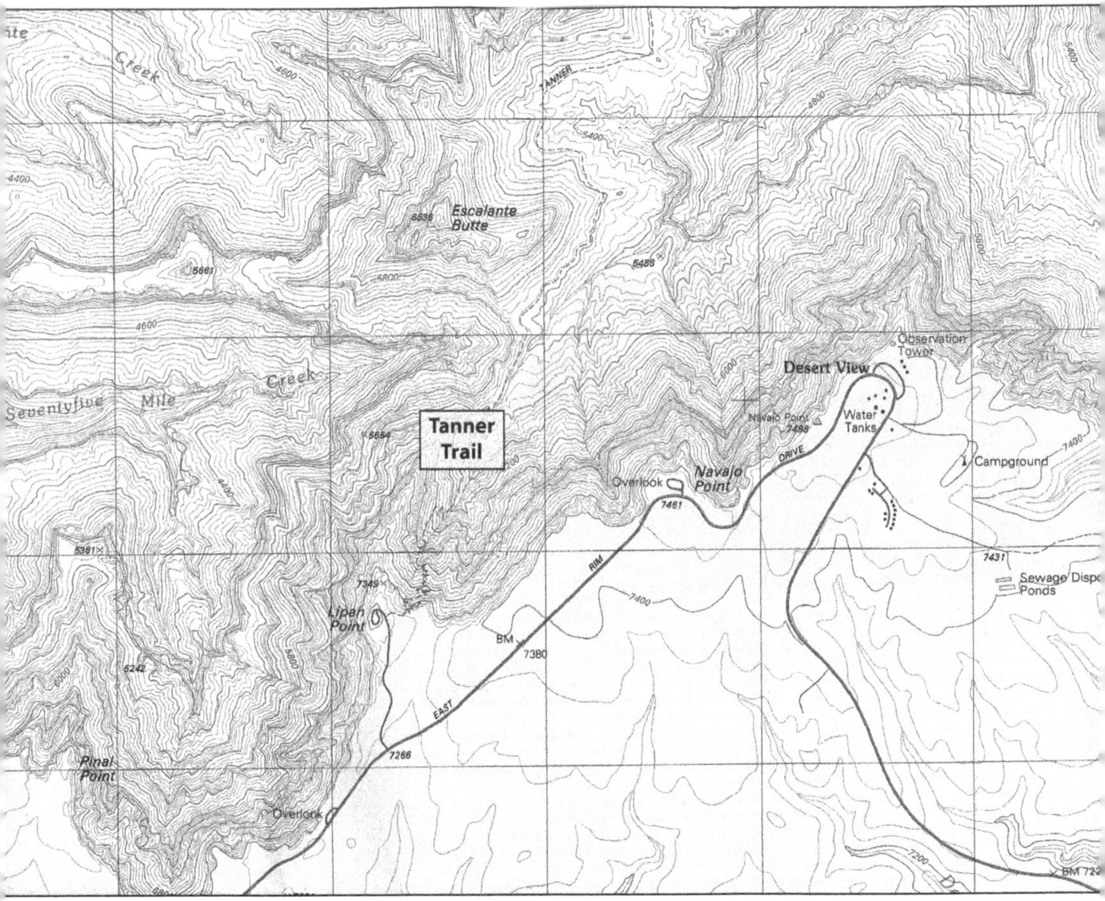

Desert View and Navajo Point, South Rim. USGS 7.5 minute series *Desert View*

Photo by Flood Hefley

Tanner Canyon. View from the Tanner Trail, which descends the South Rim at Lipan Point and travels below Desert View to the Colorado River (see above map).

Desert View is located 18 aerial miles east of the South Rim's El Tovar Hotel at an elevation of 7,438 feet. Desert View is most likely where the Spanish explorers first approached Grand Canyon in the year 1540. Spanish historian Pedro de Casteneda, of the Cardenas party, documented the area as "open to the north" where the Colorado River is extensively visible. Desert View is Grand Canyon National Park's southeast entrance area and is also the site of the Indian Watchtower.

Grand Canyoneering: The San Francisco Peaks south of the Grand Canyon were named in 1629 after St. Francis of Assisi by Franciscan missionaries who were at the Hopi villages of Oraibi. The main summits are Humphreys Peak, elevation 12,670 feet, named for General Andrew A. Humphreys; Agassiz Peak, elevation 12,340 feet, named for Swiss-American zoologist Jean Louis Agassiz; Fremont Peak, elevation 11,940 feet, named for explorer and Arizona Territorial Governor John C. Fremont. Hopi legend designates the San Francisco Peaks as the dwelling place of the *Kachinas*, their ancestral spirits.

The Echo Cliffs are located 30 aerial miles northeast of the North Rim's Grand Canyon Lodge, in the eastern park region, and is the term given by Frederick Dellenbaugh, of Major John Wesley Powell's second expedition, for the east-facing wall of Marble Canyon. With a pistol, Dellenbaugh timed the echo at twenty seconds. The elevation high is at Rock Point—5,492 feet.

Enfilade Point, located 27 aerial miles southwest of the South Rim's El Tovar Hotel, is found at an elevation of 6,160 feet above and across the Colorado River opposite the geologic formations named for the Spanish. *Enfilade* is the French military term referring to the positioning of troops and artillery prior to battle.

Eremita Mesa, located 5 aerial miles northwest of the South Rim's El Tovar Hotel at an elevation of 6,646 feet, is adjacent to Hermit Basin. The name comes from the Spanish, *eremita*, meaning "hermit."

Excalibur, located 12 aerial miles northwest of the North Rim's Grand Canyon Lodge at an elevation of 7,051 feet, is a geological mesa formation that resembles King Arthur's sword.

The Explorers Monument geological formation, located 22 aerial miles west of the North Rim's Grand Canyon Lodge, directs attention to early Grand Canyon explorers such as Major John Wesley Powell and Lieutenant Joseph Christmas Ives.

The Great Mojave Wall is the westerly cliff of **Mohave Point**, located 2 aerial miles northwest of the South Rim's El Tovar Hotel at an elevation of 6,974 feet. Along this Hermit Road section, for a time called the West Rim Drive, the descent from the rim is 1,683 feet. "Mohave" is the regional spelling of *Mojave*.

The Great Thumb Mesa is located 28 aerial miles southwest of the South Rim's El Tovar Hotel. The mesa dimensions are 3 aerial miles long by 2 aerial miles wide. The elevation gradient is 6,200 feet to 6,749 feet at **Great Thumb Point** and is descriptive of the formation's shape.

Grand Canyoneering: *Sky islands* are the Inner Canyon mesas such as Shiva Temple, Powell Plateau, Walhalla Glades, and Wotans Throne. These landmasses typically have no direct "land bridge" to the main rims and have topical areas greater than a square mile.

Hamidrik Point is located 31 aerial miles northwest of the South Rim's El Tovar Hotel at an elevation of 6,080 feet. Hamidrik is a variation of the Havasupai Indian name *Hamidreek*, meaning "nighthawk."

Mount Hayden is located 7 aerial miles northeast of the North Rim's Grand Canyon Lodge at an elevation of 8,372 feet, just below the 8,803 foot high Point Imperial, the highest North Rim overlook. The Inner Canyon steeple formation is named for Arizona Territory pioneer Charles Trumbull Hayden.

Holy Grail Temple is the United States Geological Survey's official designation for **Bass Tomb,** which is located 15 aerial miles northwest of the North Rim's Grand Canyon Lodge at an elevation of 6,703 feet. Pioneer William Wallace Bass was cremated in 1933 and his ashes distributed over this Inner Canyon formation.

Honan Point is located 6 aerial miles southeast of the North Rim's Grand Canyon Lodge at an elevation of 7,920 feet. *Honan*, sometimes spelled *honani*, is the Hopi Indian word for "badger."

Hopi Point is a promontory at an elevation of 6,985 feet located 2 aerial miles northwest of the South Rim's El Tovar Hotel. The **Hopi Wall** is the westerly cliff of Hopi Point that makes a vertical descent of approximately 1,800 feet. Hopi Point, noted for sunrise and sunset viewing, is accessed by shuttle along the Hermit Rim Road, the historic name of the road, which had also been referred to as the Hermit Road and, more recently, West Rim Drive. Hopi Point, formerly named Rowe Point for Grand Canyon pioneer Sanford Rowe, had a name change suggested by western author George Wharton James in the early 1900s. James desired to conform South Rim overlooks to Native American tribal designations.

Horseshoe Mesa is an Inner Canyon setting located 3 trail miles down the Grand View Trail and 9 aerial miles southeast of the South Rim's El Tovar Hotel. This Esplanade formation is almost a mile wide and the horseshoe arms are each a mile long. In 1900, western author George Wharton James termed the feature

"Grand View Plateau." Horseshoe Mesa is the location of Peter D. Berry's now abandoned Last Chance Mine where copper ore was once carried by burro up the Grand View Trail and brought to smelters as far away as El Paso, Texas.

Hubbell Butte, located 9 aerial miles east of the North Rim's Grand Canyon Lodge at an elevation of 6,739 feet, is named for Lorenzo Hubbell, who operated a trading post, now Hubbell Trading Post National Historic Site, at Ganado, Arizona.

Grand Canyoneering: Upon entering Grand Canyon National Park from the south, the first paved approachable overlook is Mather Point, which offers broad northerly and east-to-west views of the Inner Canyon. Directly east is the promontory of Yaki Point and the upper section of the South Kaibab Trail.

Jensen Point is located 40 aerial miles northwest of the North Rim's Grand Canyon Lodge at an elevation of 5,480 feet. Jensen Point is named for Aldus and Melissa Jensen, who operated a guided mule service utilizing David Dexter Rust's Rust Trail in 1915. Trips were also offered along the rim east and west of Bright Angel Point, twelve years before the construction of the Grand Canyon Lodge.

Jicarilla Point, located 10 aerial miles northwest of the South Rim's El Tovar Hotel, is named for Mexico's Jicarilla, meaning "little basket," Apache Indians. At an elevation of 6,400 feet, this site contains a natural arch in the westerly cliff.

Jumpup Point is located 38 aerial miles northwest of the North Rim's Grand Canyon Lodge. It is suggested that equines would have to make a series of jumps to negotiate the terrain through narrow **Jumpup Canyon.** Grand Canyon hiker Harvey Butchart was amazed to see vehicle tracks as far as the mouth of the canyon.

Kwagunt Butte is located 12 aerial miles northeast of the North Rim's Grand Canyon Lodge. At an elevation of 6,377 feet, the butte is named for the Paiute Indian, Kwagunt. While advising Major John Wesley Powell, Kwagunt said that he owned all the land in the area "because my father gave it to me."

LeFevre Overlook is located 46 aerial miles northwest of the North Rim's Grand Canyon Lodge outside Grand Canyon National Park, adjacent to U.S. Highway 89A. At an elevation of 6,436 feet, a stone and timber ramada

Grand Canyoneering: Frederick S. Dellenbaugh participated in Major John Wesley Powell's second Colorado River expedition of 1872. In his account of the journey, Dellenbaugh wrote in his *Romance of the Colorado River*:

... Each person who first looks into the abyss has a sensation of being a discoverer. *The scene is so weird and lonely and so incomprehensible in its novelty that one feels that it could never have been viewed before.*

formalizes the overlook. The LeFevre name was found etched into area trees as early as 1912 and officially cited on maps in 1927.

Lipan Point, located 16 aerial miles east of the South Rim's El Tovar Hotel at an elevation of 7,380 feet, is named for the Lipan Apache Indians. The former name of the overlook is Lincoln Point for President Abraham Lincoln.

Marsh Butte is located 7 aerial miles northwest of the South Rim's El Tovar Hotel at an elevation of 4,808 feet. Marsh Butte is named for American paleontologist Othniel Marsh, who competed with Edward Cope in the late 1880s Dinosaur Rush. The two paleontologists focused on discovery and excavation of an immense fossil field in the state of Colorado. Marsh identified eighty dinosaur species and Cope identified fifty-six. **Cope Butte** is located 4 aerial miles northwest of the South Rim's El Tovar Hotel at an elevation of 4,538 feet.

Mather Point is located 2 aerial miles northwest of the South Rim's El Tovar Hotel at an elevation of 7,129 feet. This is the first South Rim viewpoint that is encountered and that can be accessed by "mechanized travel." The overlook is

Everyone wonders what lies below. Mather point, South Rim. Photo by Flood Hefley.

named for the first director of the National Park Service, Stephen Tyng Mather. The comprehensive views include commanding north, east, and west panoramas into the Inner Canyon and Bright Angel Canyon's "The Box," the South Kaibab Trail and its descent from the Yaki Point region, and the Inner Canyon's Colorado River overlook, Plateau Point.

Grand Canyoneering: Italian for "land unknown," *Terra Incognita* was the designation of the Grand Canyon region on early 1900s maps of the United States. One could say that topographical study and cartography of the Grand Canyon started as early as 1836 when Warren A. Ferris outlined the canyon as "The Northwest Fur Country." More than twenty years later, partial map sections of the lower Colorado River region began to emerge from explorers such as Baron F.W. von Egloffstein of the 1857 Ives Expedition, and Lt. George M. Wheeler in 1871. It was Wheeler who devised the contour interval system that visually defines and measures the differences between cliffs and ridges. Wheeler also devised the quadrant map system. The quadrangle is a series of maps that make up a whole. Using compiled data between 1902 and 1923, François Matthes and Richard T. Evans executed the three-year survey work that would culminate into the 1927 Grand Canyon specific map issued by the United States Geological Survey. The 1927 map was superseded in 1962 by *Grand Canyon National Park and Vicinity, Arizona,* which used data that was collected from ground and aerial surveys between 1951 and 1962.

The Monadnock Amphitheater, at an elevation of 4,000 feet, is 14 aerial miles west of the North Rim's Grand Canyon Lodge. Monadnock is the geologic term for an isolated hill or mountain rising above a low elevation, then reduced to near sea level by a long period of erosion.

Moran Point, elevation 7,183 feet, is located 13 aerial miles southeast of the South Rim's El Tovar Hotel and is named for American landscape painter Thomas Moran. In 1873, Moran made his first Grand Canyon visit with Major John Wesley Powell to the Toroweap Overlook. He sometimes based his paintings on photographic images produced by Powell expedition member John Hillers. Western author George Wharton James desired the site name be changed to Ute Point to correspond with other tribally named formations, but the change was not made.

Mount Huethawali, located 17 aerial miles northwest of the South Rim's El Tovar Hotel at an elevation of 6,275 feet, is Havasupai for "observation place" or "white rock mountain." The mountain was formerly designated White Rock Mountain.

Navajo Point is located 17 aerial miles east of the South Rim's El Tovar Hotel. At an elevation of 7,498 feet, Navajo Point is the highest South Rim designation, as established by the United States Geological Survey. Due to the construction of the 70-foot tall Indian Watchtower at neighboring Desert View, 70 feet was added to its 7,438-foot elevation, raising that region to 7,508 feet.

End of the storm. Rainbow over O'Neill Butte (center), South Kaibab Trail. GRCA T003

O'Neill Butte, located 3 aerial miles northeast of the South Rim's El Tovar Hotel, hosts a section of the South Kaibab Trail where the route passes over the butte's southern saddle below Cedar Ridge. At an elevation of 6,072 feet, the butte is named for William Owen "Buckey" O'Neill and was formerly named The Battleship Oregon.

Grand Canyoneering: *Kaibab* is the Paiute Indian word that primarily means, "mountain lying down." The Native American term refers to the Kaibab Plateau in a way that it would appear if one might have pressed a mountain range into the ground—summit first—then removed the mountain to leave an earthly impression.

Oza Butte is located 2 aerial miles southwest of the North Rim's Grand Canyon Lodge at an elevation of 8,065 feet. Suggestive of the butte's summit, *oza* is the Paiute Indian word for "basket with a bottleneck opening."

The Painted Desert Overlook is located 6 aerial miles northeast of the North Rim's Grand Canyon Lodge on the Walhalla Plateau, which was termed the Tusayan Province by the Spanish explorers of the 1500s. The overlook is adjacent to the recently named Roosevelt Point. At an elevation of 8,429 feet, the Painted Desert Overlook offers a panoramic view of the Painted Desert, which is 9 aerial miles distant.

The Painted Desert itself is located at the Grand Canyon National Park–Navajo Indian Reservation boundary at the Little Colorado River.

The Palisades of the Desert are located 19 aerial miles east of the South Rim's El Tovar Hotel at an elevation of 6,241 feet at Palisades Creek. The Palisades are geologically referred to as "hogbacks," as the structure forms a ripple-like horizon like hogs standing in silhouette. The cliff series form the Grand Canyon's locally termed East Rim.

Pattie Butte is located 5 aerial miles northeast of the South Rim's El Tovar Hotel at an elevation of 5,306 feet. The formation is named for James Ohio Pattie who encountered the North Rim in 1826.

Plateau Point is located in the canyon at the end of the Plateau Point Trail 3 aerial miles north of the South Rim's El Tovar Hotel. At an elevation of 3,702 feet, Plateau Point had former names such as Angel Plateau, Turtle Head, and Pluto's Workshop. The overlook provides views of Granite Gorge and the Colorado River 1,360 feet below. Access is via the Bright Angel Trail, which junctions with the 1.5-mile-long Plateau Point Trail northwest of Indian Garden.

Vast interior. The Inner Canyon at Plateau Point (mid-ground) and the foot of Bright Angel Trail and the head of the River Trail. GRCA T502

Point Imperial is located 7 aerial miles northeast of the North Rim's Grand Canyon Lodge. At an elevation of 8,803 feet, Point Imperial is the highest rim overlook in Grand Canyon National Park. The former and local name of the overlook is Skidoo Point. It has been said, "Once you are done looking, all that is left to do is skidoo." Access is via the Cape Royal Road, which extends 21 miles eastward from the National Park road, which is an extension of Arizona State Highway 67 inside Grand Canyon National Park. The road section at Neal Spring, where the road forks and travels northeasterly for 3 miles to Point Imperial, is called the Point Imperial Road.

Point Retreat is where Robert Brewster Stanton made his exit from Marble Canyon, at river mile 31, after the Brown Expedition drownings. The team originally set out to assess Grand Canyon's Colorado River Inner Gorge as a possible railroad route.

> **Grand Canyoneering:** Located 4 aerial miles east of the South Rim's El Tovar Hotel, the Desert View–East Rim Drive has a moderately improved overlook that functions uniquely in the National Park. Parties may reserve Shoshone Point for functions including rim-side weddings.

Powell Plateau is located 18 aerial miles northwest of the North Rim's Grand Canyon Lodge. The 7-mile-long by 3-mile-wide "sky island" is named for Major John Wesley Powell.

Stone inlay. Powell Memorial, South Rim, 1935. GRCA 773

Powell Point is located along the Hermit Rim Road, 1 aerial mile west of the South Rim's El Tovar Hotel, at an elevation of 6,971 feet. This is the site of the Powell Memorial, which commemorates the 1869 Powell Expedition on the Colorado River. The prominent block podium does not include the crew names of the Howland brothers and William Dunn because they did not complete the journey. The site was dedicated on May 20, 1918, by National Park Service Director, Stephen Mather.

Rainbow Plateau is located 17 aerial miles northwest of the North Rim's Grand Canyon Lodge at an elevation of 7,600 feet. The plateau is remarkable for its four geologic features: Emerald, Rose, and Violet Points, and the Saffron Valley.

Red Butte is located 15 aerial miles south of the South Rim's El Tovar Hotel outside Grand Canyon National Park, adjacent to Arizona State Highway 64. The Havasupai name for the butte is *Huegadawiza* meaning "mountain of the clenched fist." The butte is geologically significant, for it is a representative of the now eroded Moenkopi Sandstone layer that once topped the Kaibab Limestone—the rim layer of Grand Canyon. **Red Butte Trail** is the one-and-one-half mile long trail that makes the ascent to the top of the lava-capped butte.

Schellbach Butte is located 5 aerial miles southwest of the North Rim's Grand Canyon Lodge. At an elevation of 6,034 feet, the butte is named for Louis Schellbach, Grand Canyon National Park's chief naturalist from 1941 to 1957. To his name is also the butterfly, Schellbach's fritillary.

Grand Canyoneering: Grand Canyon pioneer and expert Emery Kolb volunteered to assist on what would be called the Shiva Temple Expedition. Kolb was declined as a team member. Upset that his offer to help had been refused, Kolb raced ahead of the official party. He scaled the butte formation and left much evidence of his sneak preview, including a Kodak™ film package. If they ever discovered them, the team never acknowledged Emery's items.

Scorpion Ridge is located 13 aerial miles southwest of the North Rim's Grand Canyon Lodge. At an elevation of 5,836 feet, the ridge formation resembles the scorpion shape.

Shiva Temple is located 6 aerial miles southwest of the North Rim's Grand Canyon Lodge at an elevation of 7,570 feet. In 1937, media reports gave attention to a fantasy that prehistoric animals, including dinosaurs, might be marooned on Grand Canyon mesas, called sky islands. Most of the attention was focused on Shiva Temple due to the lack of land bridges to the North Rim. Funded by several hundred thousand dollars, the American Museum of Natural History of New York City organized a nine-member search team led by museum mammalogy curator, Dr. Harold E. Anthony. The team also included Grand Canyon National Park Superintendent, Minor Tillotson and naturalist, Edwin McKee. The team scaled the formation while media representatives waited for Jurassic Period news on the North Rim. Supplied by airdrops, the team examined the mesa for eleven days and only found typical modern canyon creatures and Native American artifacts.

Tiyo Point is located 4 aerial miles west of the North Rim's Grand Canyon Lodge at an elevation of 7,762 feet. Tiyo Point is named for legendary Hopi Indian Tiyo, who, legend says, survived a visit to the underworld by riding a cottonwood tree log into the Colorado River. Based on his legendary travel, Tiyo established the Snake Clan and the Snake Dance, also known as the "rain dance."

The Tonto Plateau is the expansive Inner Canyon land shelf, which is predominant on the south side of the Colorado River, where the average elevation is 3,000 feet. The plateau is named for the Tonto Apache Indians. The terrain is supported by the Tapeats Sandstone Formation, which overlies the Granite Gorge. The virtually shadeless feature, also called the Tonto Platform, extends primarily from Red Canyon in the east to Garnet Canyon in the west.

Grand Canyoneering: Granite Gorge is the Vishnu Group Formation, also called the "Grand Canyon Metamorphic Suite," consisting of the Vishnu and Brahma gneiss and Zoroaster granite cliffs that are 800' to 1,500' high. A number of geologists believe that these Inner Gorge formations are the foundational remains of an expansive alpine mountain range that has since been eroded. Based on the size and the almost vertical quality of the cliffs, it has been estimated that the peaks were capped with snow during the winter.

Trail Overlook is located .5 mile west of the South Rim's El Tovar Hotel along the Hermit Rim Road, on top of the Bright Angel Fault. Because of frequent seismic activity, earthquakes may be felt in this area. Trail Overlook, also known as Trail View Overlook, provides a commanding view of the Bright Angel Trail, Indian Garden, Grand Canyon Village, and the Kaibab National Forest.

Vista Encantada is located 5 aerial miles northeast of the North Rim's Grand Canyon Lodge at an elevation of 8,480 feet. Spanish for enchanted, the "encantada" name was changed in 1941 by Superintendent Harold C. Bryant to **Vista Encantadora.** Spanish for "enchanting," Bryant felt that *encantadora* better defined the site. On NPS and USGS maps, the site is designated as Vista Ecantada.

Walhalla Overlook is located 8 aerial miles southeast of the North Rim's Grand Canyon Lodge at an elevation of 7,994 feet. The overlook provides the classic southerly broadside view of **Angels Window** in Cape Royal's Kaibab Limestone Formation east-wing foundation.

Walhalla Plateau is located 3 aerial miles east of the North Rim's Grand Canyon Lodge and has the former name of Greenland Plateau. The plateau was renamed by topographer François Matthes. The 5-mile-wide plateau extends a heavily forested 10 miles into the Grand Canyon and is joined to the parent Kaibab Plateau by a land bridge that cradles the Cape Royal Road as it ascends to roads' end at Cape Royal.

Widforss Point is located 2 aerial miles southwest of the North Rim's Grand Canyon Lodge at an elevation of 7,882 feet. The formation is named for artist Gunnar Mauritz Widforss, who was born on October 21, 1879, in Stockholm,

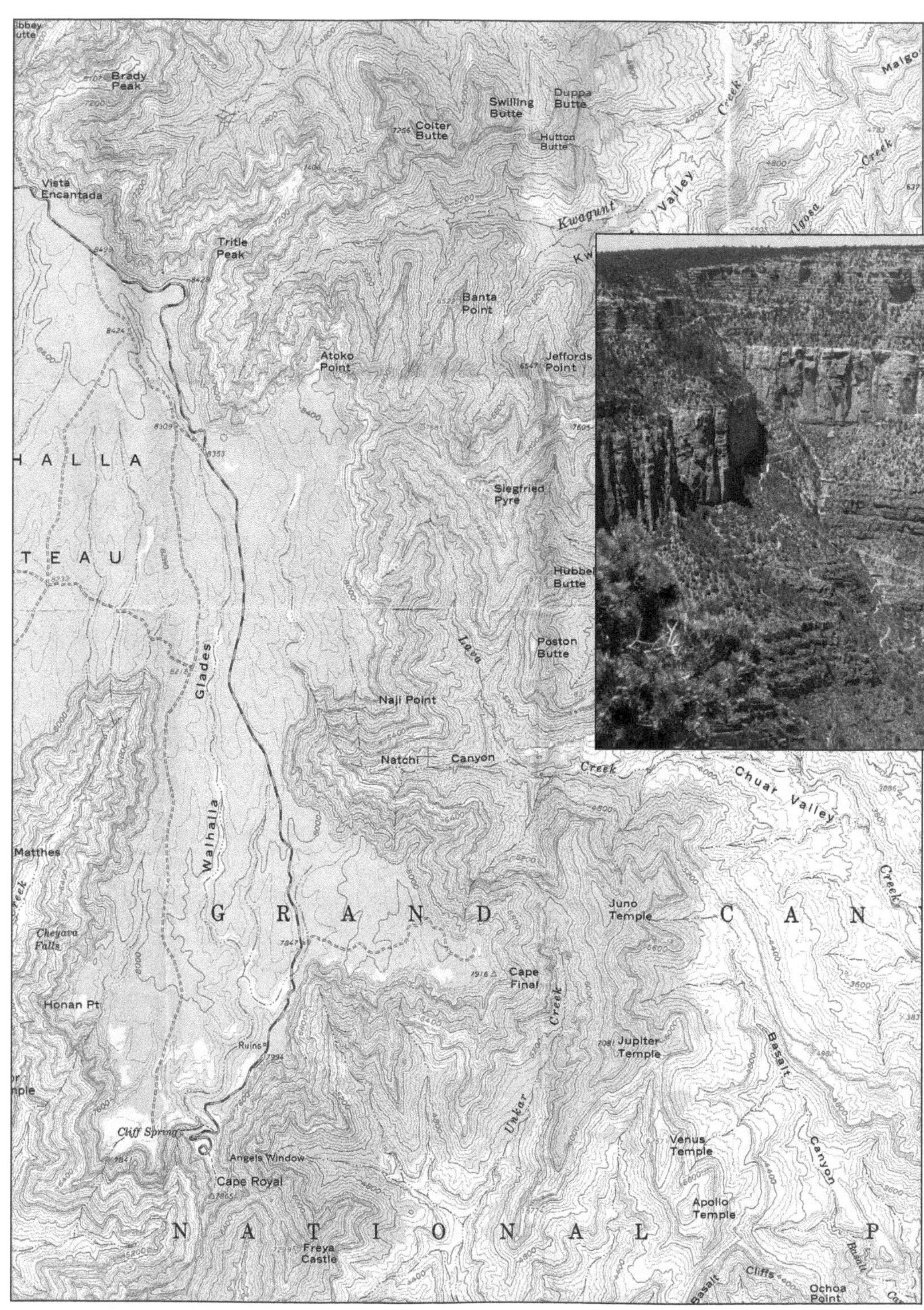

Angels Window at Cape Royal, North Rim. USGS 15 minute series *Vishnu Temple*
Inset: **Switchbacks below.** Upper Bright Angel Trail from the Rim Trail–Greenway, South Rim. Photo by Flood Hefley

Sweden, and passed away on September 30, 1934, at Grand Canyon National Park's El Tovar Hotel. Widforss came to the United States in 1921. By 1929, he became a United States citizen and earned the backing of the National Park Service Director, Stephen Mather. Widforss extensively "painted the National Parks," but it was Grand Canyon's North Rim that he most admired. In 1924, the Smithsonian Institution's National Gallery of Art in Washington, D.C. executed a one-man exhibition of Widforss' work.

Grand Canyoneering: Located at Colorado River mile 87.7, Bright Angel Canyon was formerly named Bright Angel Gorge. The canyon is 19.5 aerial miles long.

Wotans Throne is located 8 aerial miles southeast of the North Rim's Grand Canyon Lodge. The sky island is .7-mile wide by 1.5 miles long. Wotan is also called Odin and Woden. The feature was formerly named Newberry Terrace for the geologist-naturalist Dr. John Strong Newberry of the Ives Expedition of 1857–1858. Newberry was one of the first to understand the role of erosion in the formation of Grand Canyon.

Yaki Point is located 3 aerial miles east of the South Rim's El Tovar Hotel at an elevation of 7,260 feet. The formation, named for the Native American tribe of Yaqui Indians, is the South Kaibab Trail's trailhead region. It is often said, "The South Kaibab Trail starts at Yaki Point." However, the trailhead is actually south of the point at an unnamed rim contour at the Desert View–East Rim Drive's turnoff for Yaki Point.

Ranger Station:

Are there California condors in the park? The California condor is active around Grand Canyon Village, South Rim. Back in 2003, the Battleship Iowa, an Inner Canyon butte, was used by the California condor for nesting. In the time since, Grand Canyon National Park has seen many condors hatched and full-fledged in the wild through the combined efforts of the National Park Service, the Arizona Game and Fish Department, the Peregrine Fund, and the San Diego Zoo's Wild Animal Park in California, which nurtured the last 22 birds for the purpose of reintroduction into the wild at the Vermilion Cliffs of the Arizona Strip.

Ranger Station:

What are the highest Inner Canyon formations? The top five are as follows: Sullivan Peak: 8,300', Mount Hayden: 8,372', Walhalla Plateau: 8,400', Saddle Mountain: 8,424', and the highest Inner Canyon formation: Tritle Peak: 8,429'.

Photo by Flood Hefley

Sense of in*spire*-ation. Mount Hayden from the North Rim's Point Imperial.

Side Canyons

The Abyss is located along the South Rim's Hermit Road 1 aerial mile west of the South Rim's El Tovar Hotel. The Abyss is descriptive of the 1-mile-wide and 2,800-foot-deep side canyon where the rim is within feet of the Hermit Road. Stay behind the railings and easily peer down into a section of Grand Canyon from an elevation of 6,800 feet.

Grand Canyoneering: There are more than 180 side canyons, creeks, and washes that meet the Colorado River in Grand Canyon National Park. Major John Wesley Powell said of this canyon network and the side canyons that meet side canyons: *"All these canyons unite to form one Grand Canyon."*

The Main Corridor refers to the Inner Canyon area between Grand Canyon Lodge, North Rim and Grand Canyon Village, South Rim—including Bright Angel Canyon and Garden Canyon. This area also includes the Tonto Trail section located between the South Kaibab Trail and the Hermit Trail to the west and also the Colorado River and its threshold shores. All four of Grand Canyon's main trails are in this primary passage. They are the North Kaibab and South Kaibab Trails, the Bright Angel Trail, and the River Trail. These are the only trails regularly maintained by the National Park Service in Grand Canyon National Park. The Main Corridor is the Grand Canyon's deepest section—more than a mile at 6,000 feet.

Barranca, the Spanish term for "gorge," was used in 1540 as the name for Grand Canyon by Pedro de Casteneda, who served as historian under Spain's Grand Canyon discoverer, Don Garcia Lopez de Cardenas. Cardenas was led on a twenty-day roundabout march through the forest of the South Rim by Native Americans who hoped the Spanish would become discouraged by "difficulty" in reaching the canyon and simply leave the region.

The Basin, located 6 aerial miles northwest of the North Rim's Grand Canyon Lodge at an elevation of 8,246 feet, is a meadow and geological "sink" area on the North Rim. The Basin is called **Outlet Canyon** below the North Rim. Outlet Canyon acts as a North Rim conduit for relieving water accumulation at The Basin. The seasonal water that actually flows reaches **Phantom Creek,** which perennially flows into **Bright Angel Creek.**

Bass Canyon, named after Grand Canyon pioneer William Wallace Bass, is located 15 aerial miles northwest of the South Rim's El Tovar Hotel and was once formally named Trail Canyon and informally named Surprise Canyon. The Trail Canyon name comes from the high activity in the area before Grand Canyon Village was developed and before train service arrived at the South Rim. The Surprise Canyon name comes from the excitement of the tourists as they caught their first glimpse of the Grand Canyon from their arriving stagecoaches.

Grand Canyoneering: Nautiloid Canyon is a classic U-shaped valley located in Marble Canyon at river mile 34.5 and is named for the nautilus related *cephalopod,* which is fossilized into the canyon walls and floor. The nautiloid has a straight chambered-stovepipe shell and the nautilus has a chambered curved shell. There are an estimated ten billion nautiloid fossils that were trapped in a layer forty to seventy feet thick and at least 180 miles long.

Blacktail Canyon, located 25 aerial miles northwest of the North Rim's Grand Canyon Lodge, is named for area mule deer that have a tan, white, and black tail. In the early 1900s, mountain lions were systematically hunted in this prime mountain lion habitat to "protect the deer herds" and "promote the North Rim as a hunting ground." The sky island, Powell Plateau, adjoins Blacktail Canyon and is drained by the seasonal creek that flows to the west of the plateau.

The Box is located in the canyon 7 aerial miles southwest of the North Rim's Grand Canyon Lodge. The Box is designated as the 3-mile-long section of Bright Angel Canyon from the Colorado River, through the 1,200 foot high narrows of Phantom Ranch, to the area below Johnson and Jones Points. The "stunted" canyon was excavated by Bright Angel Creek, which follows Bright Angel Fault through the metamorphic Vishnu Schist Formation.

Grand Canyoneering: Named by geologist Clarence Dutton, the Transept is located immediately west of the North Rim's Grand Canyon Lodge. The rim elevation is 8,000 feet and the base of the formation is 4,400 feet. The 3,600-foot deep side canyon is easily viewed from the Grand Canyon Lodge, as the lodge is built on its rim. A transept is the feature of a cross-shaped church in which the two parts forming the arms of the cross project at right angels from the central part of the church, or nave. The Grand Canyon Transept comes from the intersection of Bright Angel Canyon and this side canyon.

Bright Angel Canyon, located on the north side of the Colorado River below the North Rim's Grand Canyon Lodge, is 19.5 miles long with the greatest width of 3.5 miles localized between Manu and Deva Temples. The head of the canyon is located at the North Rim's Neal Spring. The excavation of this major side canyon continues principally by the flow of Bright Angel Creek and its tributaries—Roaring Springs, Wall, Ribbon, and Phantom Creeks.

Brown's Canyon, located 15 aerial miles northwest of the North Rim's Grand Canyon Lodge, is named for lumber mill proprietor John F. Brown.

Burro Canyon is located 17 aerial miles northwest of the North Rim's Grand Canyon Lodge and is named for Havasupai Indian, Captain Billy Burro.

Castle Canyon is located 18 aerial miles northwest of the North Rim's Grand Canyon Lodge and is named for nearby geological formations Dox, Elaine, Freya, Guinevere, Gunther, and King Arthur Castles.

Grapevine Canyon, located 6 aerial miles east of the South Rim's El Tovar Hotel, marks the beginnings of Granite Gorge and is named for area wild grapevines.

Havasu Canyon, also called Cataract Canyon, is located 32 aerial miles southwest of the South Rim's El Tovar Hotel, adjacent to Grand Canyon National Park. The side canyon is prone to flash flooding, as it is a primary drainage path of the Kaibab-Coconino Plateau.

Hermit Basin is located below the South Rim and Hermits Rest, 4 aerial miles west of the South Rim's El Tovar Hotel, at an elevation of 5,440 feet. As referenced by western author George Wharton James in 1910, the area was noted for reclusive prospector Louis P. Brown.

The Inferno is a 3,000-foot-deep side canyon located between Mohave and Hopi Points, 1.5 aerial miles northwest of the South Rim's El Tovar Hotel. The Inferno describes the heat that rises out of the canyon.

Ranger Station:

How do hikers get across Bright Angel Creek in The Box section of Bright Angel Canyon? The Box is a narrow, steep-walled, three-mile long section of Bright Angel Canyon. It is also the location of the North Kaibab Trail near Phantom Ranch, located on the north side of the Colorado River. Before bridges were installed in the area, travelers had to make 100 wet creek crossings. The trail has since been elevated out of the creek bed with two bridges on the upper North Kaibab Trail, a bridge extending away from the North Kaibab Trail to Ribbon Falls, and four bridges over Bright Angel Creek in The Box.

Malgosa Canyon is named for Pablo de Melgosa, the Captain that Don Garcia Lopez de Cardenas dispatched during the Spanish discovery of the Grand Canyon in 1540. Melgosa was assigned the task to investigate a possible route to the Colorado River. Due to the impassable Coconino Sandstone and Redwall Limestone Formation cliffs in the vicinity of today's Desert View, Melgosa retreated with his two comrades to the South Rim. The Colorado River was too far removed from easy access to deem it worthwhile to the Spanish. The report of the river being only a few feet wide, when in actuality it is 300 feet wide, accentuated the unworthiness. Malgosa is a local spelling.

Phantom Canyon is located 6 aerial miles southwest of the North Rim's Grand Canyon Lodge in the canyon where **Phantom Creek** makes its confluence with Bright Angel Creek within The Box section of Bright Angel Canyon. The Phantom name could have been derived from the Havasupai Indian tribe's legendary ghost. However, the most likely explanation was told by architect Mary Colter. She related the story of the United States Geological Survey's François Matthes and his team, who did the majority of their cartography work from the rim in 1902. While diagramming the side canyon, the contour lines overlapped and, on paper, the canyon gradually "vanished."

Photo by Flood Hefley

Life flight. National Park Service rescue mission lifting out of Garden Creek Canyon at Indian Garden in a MD (McDonnell-Douglas) 900 Explorer Notar (no tail rotar).

Pre-flight. NPS rangers trained to perform in the rough terrain of the Inner Canyon treated and stabilized a victim before their flight out of Garden Creek Canyon to Flagstaff, Arizona.

Photo by Flood Hefley

Creeks, Springs, Waterfalls, & the Redwall-Muav Aquifer

Grand Canyoneering: In 1869, explorer Major John Wesley Powell and crew arrived at a foul-smelling side stream in Utah and named it the Dirty Devil River. In the Grand Canyon, Powell stopped at a crystal clear stream that he named Silver Creek. Later, in an expedition lecture, Powell renamed the pristine waterway Bright Angel River to counterbalance the Dirty Devil River in Utah. Afterwards, the name was modified to Bright Angel Creek.

The Redwall-Muav Aquifer, also known as the Coconino Aquifer, is the primary Grand Canyon area ground water resource and is located approximately 2,500 feet below the surface of the Coconino Plateau. The aquifer supplies the Little Colorado River to the east and Havasu Canyon to the west, where in this side canyon alone the water flows at 29,000 gallons per minute. The flow through the underplateau-system is believed to be in dynamic equilibrium—where discharge from the springs equals the aquifer recharge rate.

Bright Angel Creek is 19.5 miles long and originates 3.5 miles above the North Rim's Neal Spring where it then receives constant water. At Cottonwood Camp, halfway down the North Kaibab Trail, the creek averages 3 feet deep and 20

Fishing tackle. Park rangers planting fish from milk can at Clear Creek, ca 1940. Ironically, removal of non-native fish underway using weirs at creek entrances. GRCA 1417

Flash flood. Bright Angel Creek driving towards the Colorado River, 1966. GRCA 5104

feet wide. Before it reaches the Colorado River, Bright Angel Creek receives additional water, in an action called stream piracy, from Roaring Springs, Wall, Ribbon, and Phantom Creeks.

Bright Angel Spring was located 2 aerial miles northwest of the North Rim's Grand Canyon Lodge at an elevation of 8,160 feet. The spring was once the source of water for the North Rim. The spring was covered over by a rock slide circa 1927. North Rim facilities now had to have water pumped, or "pushed," to the rim through a pipeline from Roaring Springs, 3,000 feet below the Grand Canyon Lodge.

Grand Canyoneering: Garden Falls is located adjacent to the east side of Plateau Point where Garden Creek cascades some 750 feet before joining Pipe Creek unprecociously at the base of the Bright Angel Trail section, the Devil's Corkscrew. The upper falls is visible from the top of the Devil's Corkscrew while the remaining falls, tucked away in the rock formation that it descends, is not visible from the upper and lower trail section. Not to be confused with Columbine Falls located upstream, Garden Falls is of Garden Creek whereas Columbine Falls is of Columbine Spring.

Cheyava Falls is located 5 aerial miles northeast of the North Rim's Grand Canyon Lodge, and 9 aerial miles northeast of the South Rim's Mather Point, in the east fork of Clear Creek Canyon. The waterfall was discovered in 1903 by tour guide William Beeson, who at first perceived the water as a sheet of ice. *Cheyava* is the Hopi word best interpreted as "intermittent," as the falls do not flow continually throughout the year. The greatest display of water is during the North Rim's snow melt in spring. Cheyava is the tallest Grand Canyon National Park cascade at 1,120 feet. Source water emits from a cave that has a ceiling height of 100 feet and a shallow lake 600 feet long.

Twenty-floor plunge. Mooney Falls power-dives in Havasu Canyon, Grand Canyon System, 1938. GRCA 1210

Elves Chasm is the remote Colorado River level grotto. The grotto is fed by Royal Arch Creek, which cascades into its ponding basin. The site is frequented by river runners and by hikers accessing the backcountry area on routes that intercept the Elves Chasm Route.

Havasu Creek is a northwest-flowing Coconino Plateau subterranean river that has beginnings in the plateau underpinnings between the Grand Canyon and the Bill Williams Mountains of Williams, Arizona, 90 miles south of the canyon. In the region of the Coconino Plateau, Cataract Creek is the given name as it suggests the nature of the creek in Havasu Canyon. At the average rate of 29,000 gallons per minute, the water reveals itself in Havasu Canyon as Havasu Springs. The water contains calcium carbonate travertine like that which builds stalactites and stalagmites. The white-colored travertine coats the creek bed, which helps the creek mirror the sky's blue color and encrusts creek obstacles creating the famous pools at the ponding basins of the waterfalls.

The Waterfalls at the Havasupai Indian Reservation are downstream from the village of Supai and include the fifty-foot-high **Supai Falls,** formerly "Fifty-Foot Falls;" the seventy-five-foot-high **Navajo Falls,** for Havasupai Chief, or *kohot,* Navajo; the 100-foot-high **Havasu Falls,** formerly Bridal Veil Falls; and the tallest, the 196-foot-high **Mooney Falls** for 1880 prospector Daniel W. Mooney who on a rope descent of the falls fell to his death. Forty-foot-high **Beaver Falls,** in the Beaver Canyon cascade, is the location of the Blue Room where surface water and daylight combine to illuminate this behind the waterfall sub-stream alcove.

Water-carved crest. Havasu Falls incises Havasu Canyon, Grand Canyon System, 1938. GRCA 192

Grand Canyoneering: While scouting out the canyon in 1894, Ralph Cameron encountered a creek ahead of his partners. Cameron discovered a meerschaum pipe in the streambed and carved an early date into the pipe stem. He left the pipe to be found by his brother, Niles, and associates Pete Berry and John McClure. Finding the conspicuously placed pipe, the men wondered what circumstances brought a white man to the Inner Canyon at such an early time. When Ralph Cameron revealed the caper, Pipe Creek was named.

Monument Creek is located in the canyon 3 aerial miles northwest of the South Rim's El Tovar Hotel. Along the Tonto Trail West, the creek flows year around and is named for the 100-foot-high Tapeats Sandstone Formation pillar near the creek bed. Tapeats is the Paiute Indian who advised Major John Wesley Powell on his 1869 Colorado River expedition.

The Paria River courses from Utah's Bryce Canyon National Park and typically flows at 30 cubic feet per second into the Colorado River at Lees Ferry, Arizona. Since the construction of Glen Canyon Dam, virtually all natural materials that used to flow from the northeast through the canyon are deposited behind the dam. With the Little Colorado River and Kanab Creek to the west, the Paria is one of the three main waterways that can contribute the sediment that supports eroded Grand Canyon beach habitats. The Paiute Indians call the river *Pahreah*, meaning "water deer" or "water elk."

Phantom Creek is located 6 aerial miles southwest of the North Rim's Grand Canyon Lodge in the canyon and makes a confluence with Bright Angel Creek within The Box section of Bright Angel Canyon.

Pipe Creek is located in the canyon 3 aerial miles northeast of the South Rim's El Tovar Hotel. At the base of the Bright Angel Trail's Devil's Corkscrew section at their tributary junction, Pipe Creek receives the water of Garden Creek. Pipe Creek Narrows is a 1.5-mile-long slot segment of Pipe Creek that is also encountered at the base of the Devil's Corkscrew.

Pumpkin Spring is located at river mile 212 and is descriptive of the 30-foot diameter by 20-foot high travertine "pumpkin-shaped bowl" that drips bitter water into the Colorado River.

Ribbon Falls (elevation 3,750 feet), **Upper Ribbon Falls** (elevation 4,400 feet), and **Upper Upper Ribbon Falls** (elevation 5,800 feet), are located in an Inner Canyon "bay" side canyon adjacent to the North Kaibab Trail. The 175-foot-high Ribbon Falls includes a moss-covered travertine "cone" base and a shallow ponding basin. The waterfall's configuration allows passage behind the cascade. Introduced here, **Ribbon Falls Alcove** is an exposed stalactite and stalagmite formation-in-progress natural feature, which has in the making one complete stalactite and stalagmite formation, one tapering column that will eventually join the alcove floor, and a ceiling to floor seep with a collection basin.

Roaring Springs is adjacent to the North Kaibab Trail and cascades 400 feet from the source in the Muav Limestone Formation creating Roaring Springs Creek. Access to the base of the spring is via the Roaring Springs Trail, a .3 mile spur route from the North Kaibab Trail. *Muav* is the Paiute Indian word meaning "saddle." Roaring Springs is the domestic water source for the North and South Rims and the Inner Canyon–Main Corridor campgrounds and rest houses.

Grand Canyoneering: In 1908, Ellsworth Kolb traveled to Cheyava Falls from Phantom Ranch, at the time called Rust's Camp. Ellsworth described the cave's ceiling as "100 feet high" and the floor as a "600-foot-long lake." Subsequently, his brother Emery traveled by boat down the Colorado River to the mouth of Clear Creek and followed the streambed to the falls. In 1930, the Kolb Brothers traveled together to the top of the falls from the North Rim. To do this, the brothers left the edge of the canyon 6 aerial miles southeast of today's Grand Canyon Lodge. At an elevation of 7,920 feet, near Honan Point (Hopi for "badger"), the brothers descended into the canyon 2,080 feet to the crest of the falls where they determined that there is at least a little water year around.

Tapeats Creek is located 24 aerial miles northwest of the North Rim's Grand Canyon Lodge. After flowing 3 of 5 miles to the Colorado River, Tapeats Creek receives the water of Thunder River. Tapeats retains creek status even though it carries an increased volume gained from Thunder River.

Thunder River is located 33 aerial miles west of the North Rim's Grand Canyon Lodge. Thunder River is called "one of the shortest rivers in the world" and begins from spring sources 3,600 feet below the North Rim at 3,000 foot deep **Thunder River Cave.** At the source, the stream is in the form of **Thunder River Falls,** which cascades and courses eastward for .5 mile, then joins Tapeats Creek. Timp Point, located 22 aerial miles northwest of the North Rim's Grand Canyon Lodge at an elevation of 7,640 feet, is the only known overlook on the Kaibab Plateau where it is possible, with binoculars, to view Thunder River at the source on the north wall of Tapeats Canyon.

Grand Canyoneering: Indian Lake is located 14 aerial miles north of the North Rim's Grand Canyon Lodge at an elevation of 8,722 feet. Positioned outside of Grand Canyon National Park in the DeMotte Park of the North Kaibab Ranger District, this rare pond-like lake has the ability to retain water, which is important to wildlife on the limestone and sandstone-based Kaibab Plateau, where typically rain water and snow melt percolate immediately into the substratum.

Vasey's Paradise is a cascade that flows into the Colorado River at river mile 32. The aquifer produces 4,000 gallons of water per minute that emit from 12,000 feet of passageways. Naming the cascade in the honor of the United States Department of Agriculture's Dr. George Vasey, Major John Wesley Powell entered in his diary:

The river turns sharply east, and seems inclosed by a wall, set with a million brilliant gems. On coming nearer, we find fountains bursting from the rock ... and the spray in the sunshine forms the gems which bedeck the wall. The rocks below are covered with mosses, and ferns, and many beautiful flowering plants. We name it Vasey's Paradise, in honor of the botanist who traveled with us last year.

Time-out. Where hikers retire in the middle of summer days. Ribbon Falls, North Kaibab Trail. Photo by Flood Hefley

Ranger Station:

What happened to Havasupai waterfalls after the flood of August 2008? They are very different compared to the 2008 pre-flood conditions. Sadly, Navajo Falls is gone. In place of Navajo Falls is a new waterfall called by the tribe New Navajo Falls. Havasu Falls spills to the immediate west of its former course, and the ponding basin has filled about 40% with earth. Mooney Falls spills very similar to its former course, and the ponding basin is almost completely full of earth. Havasu Creek, after making its Mooney Falls descent, flows against the easterly base of the cliff and exits its bay. A newly formed waterfall, the tribally named Rock Falls, a broad-crested, 50-foot high falls, is located between the village of Supai and Havasu Falls.

Ranger Station:

Where do hikers get water along the North Bass Trail? The 14-mile route is among the longest named backcountry routes in the canyon. Even though reliable water sources may dry up from year to year, and have been known to fade away in-between years, the renewable water sources on which hikers rely while traveling the North Bass Trail are, occurring from the trailhead to the end of the trail, Muav Saddle Spring, White Creek, Shinumo Creek, and the Colorado River.

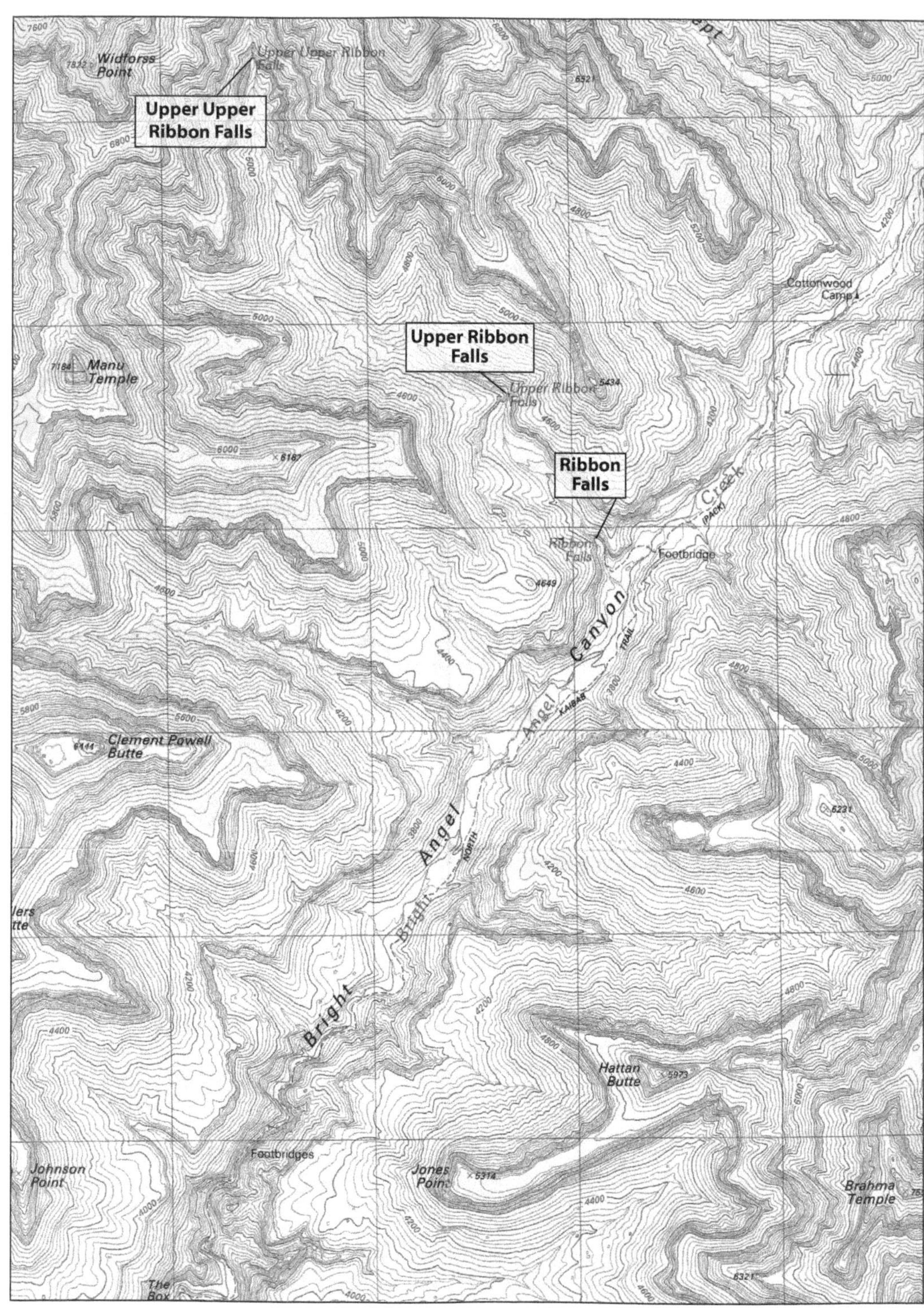

Ribbon Falls, Upper Ribbon Falls, and Upper Upper Ribbon Falls above Bright Angel Canyon's The Box. Lower North Kaibab Trail. USGS 7.5 minute series *Bright Angel Point.*

The Colorado River, Rapids, and River Runners

The River

Oar power. Float trip on the Colorado River below Havasu Creek. GRCA D3767

The Colorado River flows 277 miles through Grand Canyon. From Lees Ferry, Arizona, to the Grand Wash Cliffs, the river descends 2,200 feet, losing much of its elevation at the end of some 100 rapids. The greatest known depth of the river, or *thalweg* (a bowed imaginary line following the deepest part of a stream), of 110 feet was measured by hydrologist Luna Leopold, son of Aldo Leopold, at river mile 114 near the mouth of Garnet Canyon, 19 aerial miles northwest of

> **Grand Canyoneering:** The Colorado River has several Native American names including the Havasupai, *Hakatai*, meaning "loud sound;" from the Diné (Navajo), *Pocketto*, meaning "powerful;" and from the Paiute, *Pahaweap*, meaning "river far down."

the South Rim's El Tovar Hotel. As determined by the United States Geological Survey, the narrowest river section is **Granite Narrows** and occurs at river mile 135, between Tapeats Rapids and Deer Creek Falls, where the river flows at 75 feet wide.

Before the construction of **Glen Canyon Dam,** the river was able to transport great amounts of natural debris including rock, dirt, uprooted trees, and house-sized boulders. In years of severe winter and resultant snow melt-off, the supercharged river was able to move at a rate of some 250,000 cubic feet per second. This volume is more than twice as much compared to an average pre-dam spring flood of 80,000 to 100,000 cubic feet per second. Geologist **Gene Shoemaker** described cubic feet per second as that number of basketballs passing a fixed point every second. During the twenty-four-hour period of September 13, 1937, the river at flood conditions carried 27,600,000 tons of debris past the United States Geological Survey's river level gauging stations where the river was naturally width-restricted at the Kaibab Suspension Bridge east of Bright Angel Creek. During any twenty-four-hour period, on an average day, more than 500,000 tons of debris moved past the stations. In relationship to Hoover Dam, these gauging towers are defined as Grand Canyon Station, as they anticipated the quantity of water and material flowing into Lake Mead at the site of the dam.

The river also flowed a muddy red. The catch phrase of the Colorado once was, "Too thick to drink and too thin to plow." Presently the river flows an emerald green when its tributary streams are not depositing sediment under their own flood conditions. The cold and clear water released from Lake Powell, 45 to 55 degrees F. year around, is virtually free of sediment, which fosters a denser growth of more than fifty species of algae—particularly *cladophora glomerata,* one of the more aggressive algae. Over the river system within Grand Canyon National Park, algae's greatest growth density is in the first 75 miles below Glen Canyon Dam.

Currently the river flows at the rate of 8,000 to 16,000 cubic feet per second as a daily high depending on hydroelectric needs. As the river has fluctuated in depth due to these needs, a high water mark stain is left behind and is commonly called "the bathtub ring." River exploration in the Grand Canyon systematically began in 1869 with Major John Wesley Powell and his nine-member crew. At the present time, the National Park Service monitors commercial and noncommercial river running for sport.

Grand Canyoneering: Distances on the Colorado River are measured in river miles, which account for waterway "bends" and "meanderings" from Lees Ferry, Arizona, through Grand Canyon to Lake Mead at Pearce's Ferry. Officially cited as River Mile Zero, Lees Ferry is located 4.5 river miles eastward of the National Park and is the start of all miles measured through Grand Canyon. The lower-lying landscape within this area of vertical cliffs is locally termed The Gap. This depression in the land affords passage from rim-to-rim and provides for the only possible access to river level by mechanized travel between Glen Canyon and Grand Canyon.

Grandness of the Canyon. Colorado and Little Colorado River confluence from the Cape Solitude wilderness. GRCA D1730

The Little Colorado River flows above and below ground for some 300 miles from its source in the White Mountains of eastern Arizona. The Little Colorado River makes a confluence with the Colorado River in Grand Canyon National Park in the area below Cape Solitude, 21 aerial miles southeast of the South Rim's El Tovar Hotel. The underground stream, the Redwall-Muav Aquifer, is a primary water contributor to the Grand Canyon system as it emits as Blue Springs in the Little Colorado River Gorge.

An assemblage of canyons and river drainages establishes the relationship of Grand Canyon National Park and Utah's Bryce Canyon and Zion National Parks. The Paria River drains Bryce Canyon and then joins the Colorado River at Lees Ferry, Arizona. The Virgin River drains Zion and then joins the Colorado in Lake Mead.

Revival. Restoration of the Kolb Brothers' boat, the *Edith*. GRCA

Green River, Utah and Wyoming, are the historic embarkation sites for Colorado River runners through Grand Canyon. Major John Wesley Powell's planned embarkation point from Green River, Wyoming, coincided with the completion of the Trans Continental Railroad just fourteen days before his boats

Safe landing at Boat Beach. Located on the outskirts of Phantom Ranch at the mouth of Bright Angel Creek, Boat Beach reflects the loss of beach habitats throughout Grand Canyon. The massive sand deposit that the river runners were standing on in 1977 is now gone—stripped away by the river. Their boats are true "baloney boats," five military outrigger pontoons first lashed together in 1961 by Jack Currey, founder of Western River Expeditions. Currey had ordered two railroad boxcars of pontoons—one full of oblong-shaped rafts and one loaded with outrigger pontoons to be lashed on each side of an oblong raft. When the supplies were delivered, Currey was dismayed to find two boxcars full of outrigger pontoons. With a commercial trip nearing and not enough time to correct the blunder, he made rafts entirely out of outrigger pontoons. From this, the J-Rig was invented, preferred, and patented. Boats of today are specifically engineered for the purpose of running rivers. Notice Bright Angel Pueblo adjacent to the North Kaibab Trail. Photo by Rye Hefley, inset photo by Flood Hefley

were delivered by train to the Wyoming site. River runners today must start as close as Lees Ferry, Arizona, due to the presence of Glen Canyon Dam 15 river miles upstream. Green River, Utah (formerly Blake, Utah), is 155 aerial miles north of Glen Canyon Dam, and Green River, Wyoming, is 180 aerial miles north of the Utah site.

Grand Canyoneering: Representatives of the states affected by the Colorado River System signed the *Colorado River Compact* at Santa Fe, New Mexico. There the state-to-state water allocation was set for Wyoming, Colorado, New Mexico, Utah, Arizona, Nevada, California, and the country of Mexico. The first claim filed on Colorado River water was made in 1877 by Thomas Blythe, who diverted a portion of the river to irrigate fields in California.

Lees Ferry was established on December 25, 1871, by John Doyle Lee, 4.5 river miles upstream from Grand Canyon National Park. The ferry service became the most practical Colorado River crossing until the completion of the Navajo Bridge in 1929, located 4.5 river miles downstream from the ferry in Marble Canyon. The first boat used for ferry service was the *Nellie Powell*, which was abandoned by Major John Wesley Powell. Later, a barge system was implemented that could handle the portage on an automobile. The cost to cross the Colorado River was three dollars—a large sum of money in that time period.

The Rapids

In the Colorado River's confined descent through the canyon, it loses a dramatic amount of elevation in the form of rapids. Descent through the rapids is steep. About half of the river's total drop takes place in the rapids that make up about ten percent of the river's length.

Rating the turbulence of the river rapids in North America is based on a scale of "One-to-Six" where the six rating provides the greatest challenge. The Grand Canyon, however, uses a different rating scale, in which rapids are rated on a scale of one to ten. The reason, as Western River Expeditions explains, is to "accommodate such a wide variety of rapids and river variances." A rapid with a ten rating suggests a fifty-fifty chance of a successful run—passage without capsizing. Approximately 100 rapids occur in Grand Canyon National Park. Some of the more difficult rapids include Fossil Rapid and Soap Creek, rated "six;" Sockdolager and Grapevine, rated "seven;" Badger Creek, Duebendorff, Granite Rapid, Hance Rapid, Hermit, and Upset, rated "eight;" Horn Creek, rated "nine;" and Crystal Rapid and Lava Falls, rated "ten."

Drowning in the rapids often occurred in the historic Colorado River. Before the construction of Glen Canyon Dam, the river carried great amounts of suspended sediment. After a boat capsized in a rapid, boaters were in immediate danger of drowning due to the weight of silt filling their clothes. As just one example, three men assigned to the Navajo Bridge project of 1929 drowned at Lees Ferry when their boat capsized. Arizona Highway Department engineer W.R. Hutchins reported, *An accident meant disaster to even an expert swimmer.... The heavy silt content of the river water immediately makes a sand bag of ones clothing and drags him down.*

> **Grand Canyoneering:** *In order to run the rapids, you have to start the boat upside down. Because when you finished, the boat's right side up... that's how you run rapids.*
>
> —BUS HATCH, retold by Don Hatch of *Hatch River Expeditions*

Crystal Rapid, located at river mile 98, was altered by massive debris flows from the historic flood of December 5, 1966 and once again in 1983. In these years, the former low-grade rapid changed overnight into one of the toughest sections of white water not only in the canyon, but also in North America, as debris rushed down **Crystal Canyon** and pushed the river to the south bank. Anyone floating the river the next day rounded the bend at river mile 98 and were first unpreparedly greeted by the sound, and then the sight, and then the ride of a new and large rapid. **Crystal Lake** is the term given by river runners to the water that pools behind the rapid.

Debris flows are a mixture of water, rock, and soil pulled by gravity. Debris flows can range from small to massive surfaces that can collect boulders, plants, and trees that thunder down side canyons usually after a sudden and prolonged heavy rain.

Lava Falls Rapid is located 179 river miles downstream from Lees Ferry, Arizona. The rapid is considered one of the two most difficult rapids not only on the Colorado River in Grand Canyon but, like Crystal Rapid, also in North America. Like Crystal Rapid, Lava Falls rates a "ten" on the river rating scale. The name Lava Falls is derived from its location in the volcanic region of Toroweap. The alternate name is Vulcan Rapid. In the rapid, "The Ledge Hole" is caused by a course of basalt boulders deposited by a debris flow that traveled down Prospect Canyon. The river water that pools behind the rapid is termed **Lava Lake** by river

Photo by Flood Hefley

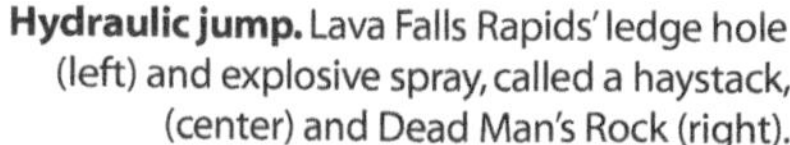

Hydraulic jump. Lava Falls Rapids' ledge hole (left) and explosive spray, called a haystack, (center) and Dead Man's Rock (right).

Swamped. Oar-powered boat running Lava Falls Rapid. GRCA D3801

runners. **Dead Man's Rock** is a lava boulder located in the Lava Falls Rapid. The boulder is positioned at the north bank, called "river right," where the river's current drives boats into contact once on that side of the river. In his river expedition diary of 1869, Major John Wesley Powell documented the dormant volcano, Vulcan's Throne, which is positioned directly on the North Rim:

> *A cinder cone, or extinct volcano, stands on the very brink of the canyon. What a conflict of water and fire there must have been here! Just imagine a river of molten rock running down into a river of melted snow. What a seething and boiling of the water; what a cloud of steam rolled into the heavens!*

Grand Canyoneering: Most of the Colorado River rapids in Grand Canyon are formed by flash flooding side canyons that deliver debris to river level—as in the case of Crystal Rapid at river mile 98, which was bulldozed to the river's south bank. In some cases, such as President Harding Rapid located at river mile 43.7, *slumping* formed the rapid. Slumping is a rock mass that sheers off by its own weight and falls from the parent wall.

Bright Angel Creek Delta is located 7 aerial miles southwest of the North Rim's Grand Canyon Lodge, where the delta is bisected by Bright Angel Creek and joins the Colorado River. The delta is the result of prehistoric and modern debris flows that traveled down Bright Angel Canyon. The .5-mile long shoreline continues to erode faster than it is replenished by the Colorado River's tributary streams, as a direct result of Glen Canyon Dam. The dam retains the beach-forming rehabilitative sediment that not only formerly flowed through the canyon, but flowed through with power. As a contributing factor, Bright Angel Creek's wire-mesh-covered banks

Displacing the river. From the Escalante Route, Unkar Delta pushes the Colorado River to its southern bank. GRCA D1755

do not allow the creek to make a 100 percent deposit. Historically, the delta extended 600 feet from its head to its progression into the Colorado River At the Bright Angel Creek Delta, **Boat Beach,** also called Boater's Beach, is the designated minimum impact mooring strand for commercial and private river craft. Here, river runners and river guides can access the supplies of Phantom Ranch.

Granite Gorge is composed of metamorphic and igneous rock and channels the Colorado River through the canyon from Grapevine Creek at river mile 81 to the Hundred and Forty Mile Canyon at river mile 140. The gorge sections include Stephen Aisle, Conquistador Aisle, Middle Granite Gorge, and Granite Narrows.

Gathering currents. Bright Angel Creek rushes through its cobblestone delta to join the Colorado River at river mile 87.5.

Sentinel Rock is an alternate name for **Ten Mile Rock,** which is a vertically placed boulder slab that fell from the rim area of Marble Canyon and stands out of the Colorado River 10 river miles downstream from Lees Ferry.

Conquistador Aisle is the Colorado River section located 23 aerial miles northwest of the South Rim's El Tovar Hotel. The designated geological terrace sites positioned above the Colorado River are named for the Spanish explorers Alarcon, DeVaca, Garces, and Tobar (Tovar).

Christmas Rapid is also known as Waltenberg Rapid. On United States Geological Survey maps, the name is misspelled as Walthenberg. On Christmas Eve, 1911, the Kolb Brothers, Ellsworth and Emery, capsized and damaged their boats on their historically filmed trip. The men repaired the boats on Christmas Day.

Horn Creek Rapid is located at the mouth of Horn Creek Canyon, 2 aerial miles north of the South Rim's El Tovar Hotel. The canyon and rapid are named for frontier scout Tom Horn. In a river boat crossing attempt on February 20, 1929, the first Grand Canyon National Park naturalist, Glen Sturdevant and National Park Service rangers Fred Johnson and James Brooks started across the river upstream from the rapid to run to the opposite bank. The river's current carried the boat too far downstream into the rapid where the boat capsized. Sturdevant and Johnson drowned while Brooks escaped to the safety of Phantom Ranch. In commemoration, located side-by-side 5 aerial miles southwest of the North Rim's Grand Canyon Lodge, are **Sturdevant Point,** elevation 5,331 feet, and **Johnson Point,** elevation 5,295 feet.

Grand Canyoneering: A question that often arises, "Did Bessie Hyde become river guide Georgie White?" Upon White's passing in 1992, Georgie's close friends assessed her personal affects. Found in her dresser were a handgun, like that of the Hydes, and Glen and Bessie's marriage license. Some say they wouldn't put it past Georgie to leave behind "Bessie clues" to keep folks speculating. Georgie loved a good story. Based on photographs and other evidence, it can be concluded that the women were not the same person. The evidence says, "no," but the details of the mystery are intriguing—for one thing, Georgie's given first name is ... Bessie.

The River Runners

River runners on the Colorado River in Grand Canyon numbered less than 200 between 1869 and 1950. Early river runners who approached the Colorado for adventure include E.B. (Elias Benjamin) "Hum" Wooley with John King and Arthur Sanger, who in 1903 used Wooley's homemade boat; Charles Russell and Edwin Monett, who floated from Green River, Utah, to California's Needles Mountains in 1909; Nathaniel Galloway with Julius Stone in 1909; Ellsworth and Emery Kolb, who made their commercially successful film in 1911; and the honey-

Grand Canyoneering: Martin Litton is the Colorado River runner who established the commercial Grand Canyon Dories, a minimum impact mode of river travel through the canyon system. Litton named his non-motorized wooden boats, which were based on the design of the Grand Banks fishing dory, after wilderness areas that were negatively altered by man. One of Martin's boats, *Music Temple*, is a Glen Canyon formation named by Major John Wesley Powell that is now under the waters of Lake Powell.

Rough sea tempered. *Music Temple* in the courtyard of the original Visitor Center, 1984. Martin Litton adopted the Grand Banks fishing dory design to handle the toughest Grand Canyon rapids. GRCA 13633

mooners, Glen and Bessie Hyde, who went missing without a trace, possibly losing their lives in 1928.

Glen and Bessie Hyde "honeymooned" in the Grand Canyon and ran the Colorado River rapids. Using a sweep-scow, a wide beam rowboat with large oars at the bow and stern, the couple began their journey at Green River, Utah. They astonishingly passed many rough rapids and reached the Bright Angel Creek in twenty-eight days. With the boat moored, the Hydes' hiked to the South Rim where they spoke with Emery Kolb. With regard to the rapids still ahead of Glen and Bessie, Kolb encouraged them to take and use his life jackets. After refusing to use his jackets, they returned to their boat. Emery took the last photograph of the pair as they started down the trail. Evidence suggests that they drowned in the Colorado River at the class 4 to 7-rated 232 Mile Rapid on November 28, 1928. What actually happened is not known. Their bodies were never recovered despite extensive searches of the river and side canyons. Five river miles downstream from the 232 Mile Rapid, the Hydes' boat was found fully intact. Left behind also was Bessie's personal book of poetry.

Albert "Bert" Loper, also known as "The Old Man of the River," shared in the early pioneering of the Colorado River in 1907 with fellow boatmen Charles Russell and Edwin Monett. Loper ran the river in 1939 and again ten years later before passing away just before his 80th birthday on the river due to an apparent heart attack at the 24½ Mile Rapid on July 8, 1949.

Derelict vessel. The Bert Loper constructed metal boat used by Charles Russell and August Tadje, the *Ross Wheeler*. GRCA 17108B

The *Ross Wheeler* is located on the south bank of the Colorado River at river mile 108. The beached metal boat was built in 1914 by Bert Loper, who named it after a friend who was killed in a fight. The boat was wrecked in 1915 by Charles Russell and August Tadje. The historic boat, under the protection of the National Park Service, is secured to the river bank to protect it from high water.

Haldane "Buzz" Holmstrom became the first authenticated solo Grand Canyon river runner in 1937. Holmstrom embarked from Green River, Wyoming, in October and in seven weeks reached the newly constructed Hoover Dam—completed in 1936. Buzz Holmstrom used a 15-foot-long boat that he not only designed, but fashioned out of cedar that he himself milled.

Amos Burg was the first to run the Colorado River through Grand Canyon in an inflatable boat. From Green River, Wyoming, Burg embarked on August 26, 1938, accompanied by Haldane "Buzz" Holmstrom and Bill Johnson, who floated the river in a cedar boat. They completed their trip at Lake Mead on November 6, 1938.

Stern-first rapid-running. At Bright Angel Creek, Norman Nevills and his Nathaniel Galloway–based cataract boat, The *WEN*, 1947. GRCA 1584

Norman Davies Nevills was the first boatman to establish the river running guide business that would ultimately pioneer Colorado River tourism through the Grand Canyon. From 1938 to 1949, Nevills operated Mexican Hat Expeditions, based at Mexican Hat, Utah. Nevills' first commercial trip was for the University of Michigan, when he and partner Laphene "Don" Harris guided botany professor Elzada Clover and students Lois Jotter (the first women to float the entire length of the river in Grand Canyon) and Eugene Atkinson for the purpose of botanical identification. The trip started on June 20, 1938. After floating from Green River, Utah, Atkinson departed at Lees Ferry, Arizona—the beginning of Grand Canyon. After the examination of the Colorado River's riparian flora in the canyon, the remaining party arrived forty days later at Lake Mead. Norman's famous boat, the *WEN*, is named for his father William Eugene Nevills. The lives of Norman and his wife Doris were tragically lost on September 19, 1949, when their Piper airplane malfunctioned and crash-landed at Mexican Hat.

Alexander "Zee" Grant was the first to kayak the Colorado River's Grand Canyon rapids in 1941. Using a double-bladed oar, Grant traveled from Green River, Utah, to Lake Mead. The kayak, *Escalante*, had a stretched canvas outer covering much like that of the Eskimo's stretched skin design. Grant was accompanied by Norman Nevills, who traveled in the Mexican Hat cataract boat, the *WEN*.

Tiny plastic boat. Otis "Dock" Marston swamping through Mile 217 Rapid in the 7-foot long Sportyak II, 1963. GRCA 5008

River historian Otis "Dock" Marston with Ed Hudson became the first boatmen to pilot a powerboat through Grand Canyon in 1949. Aboard Hudson's *Esmeralda II*, the boatmen embarked from Lees Ferry and reached Lake Mead in less than five days. In 1950, Marston repeated the journey in a Chris-Craft powerboat. The *Esmeralda II* was named after the 1850s sternwheeler, *Esmeralda*, which was piloted by Captain Thomas Trueworthy, who hauled freight in the region of the lower Colorado River.

Jim and Bob Rigg set an oar-powered speed record in a Norman Nevills Mexican Hat cataract boat in 1951. A non-motorized trip is typically twelve to fourteen days long. On the Colorado River, the Riggs traveled the 225 river miles from Lees Ferry to Diamond Creek in less than two days. **Diamond Creek** is the common exit point for Colorado River excursions. To access the Colorado River at Diamond Creek, tour companies transport patrons and equipment under a Hualapai Indian Reservation-use permit.

Bill Beer and John Daggett swam the entire length of the Colorado River in Grand Canyon in the spring of 1955. The 280-river mile trip, from Lees Ferry to Pearce Ferry, was the idea of their friend John Bursell. The notion was predicated on how dangerous it would be to swim the Colorado River in Grand Canyon. The untamed river rapids were deafening and beat the duo against the rocks and boulders in the river channel. Sitting down in the river at eye level limited vision and planning. The partners would disappear from sight as one another would descend downstream below the naturally occurring pool of water, often called a lake, before each rapid. In one occurrence, Daggett was trapped under a boulder in

President Harding Rapid in Marble Canyon. Their "waterproof" military neoprene packs, used for supply storage and to aid in floatation, performed poorly at holding out the 55 degree F. river water. Hypothermia was a constant threat. Beer and Daggett had waded into the river at Lees Ferry and successfully swam through the Grand Canyon in twenty-six days. The entire venture, including transportation, equipment, and food, which was cooked in a skillet over open driftwood fires, cost $150. The National Park Service now prohibits swimming the Grand Canyon National Park section of the Colorado River.

Grand Canyoneering: Diamond Creek is also known as "Truck Stop." Flash floods down this side canyon have swept river expedition vehicles, which haul rafts and supplies, into the Colorado River.

Harry Aleson was the first to attempt Colorado River upstream runs for sport in 1941. These "wrong way runs" were unsuccessful due to Aleson's underpowered boats. In 1938, Harry Aleson lived in a cave in western Grand Canyon's Quartermaster Canyon. Aleson was also the one who encouraged Georgie White to establish her river running business, which utilized military surplus rafts.

Georgie White was the first woman to navigate the Colorado River in Grand Canyon. White pioneered the use of United States Army surplus rafts to start her commercial river running business. Georgie White bought the rafts "for a song" in 1955 with river runner Harry Aleson. The inspiration for using these big rafts possibly came from Aleson and White's 1946 float trip, in which they went through the rapids on a driftwood raft. Surely their 1947 trip, in which they used army surplus rafts, solidified the boat of choice on the river. White's humongous neoprene constructed pontoon rafts were often called, interchangeably, Baloney Boats, Thrill Rigs, or, for Georgie, G-Rigs. Based on tourist volume, her River Rat outfit permitted low prices, which she called, "The Share the Expense Plan." Georgie's innovation and personal standing earned her the nickname "Woman of the River." The big boats accommodated dozens of river running customers at one time. These large boats also eliminated portaging—

Baloney Boat. Georgie White's Triple Rig Raft near Matkatamiba Rapid, Colorado River mile 148.5, 1964. GRCA 4610A

carrying a boat around a rapid, or lining a boat—the process of bypassing a rapid by ushering a boat down the river's bank with a rope that is tied to the craft while the other end is held by hand at the shore. Powered by Johnson outboard motors, some rafts were lashed three abreast for what Georgie felt would improve safety on the river. Even today, all river running ventures have their individual risks. One day on the river, one of Georgie's boats came into contact with a rapid broadside. As the boat progressed to the crest of the rapid, the boat folded in half and collapsed on itself and passengers.

Grand Canyoneering: With the commencement of construction on Glen Canyon Dam, the movement of watercraft on the Colorado River would be forever interrupted. River runners would no longer be able to float Glen Canyon prior to their Grand Canyon run. The fundamental beginnings of building a dam, such as diverting the river around the construction site, took the place of a boat passing from Glen Canyon to Grand Canyon. Lees Ferry, also called "Lonely Dell," "Pahreah Crossing," and "River Mile Zero," would become the designated launch site, or "put-in," for the approximately 4,000 boats launched annually at Marble Canyon.

Turbojet engine boats *Kiwi*, *Wee Red*, *Wee Yellow*, and *Dock* (for boatman Otis "Dock" Marston) were the boats that made the first and only complete wrong way run on the Colorado River in Grand Canyon. In July of 1960, the greatest challenge to succeed in the upstream run would be to pass the boats through Lava Falls Rapid, at river mile 179, with the 185 horsepower engines. After 100 attempts, Jon Hamilton persistently drove his boat for ninety minutes at the tail of Lava Falls and finally achieved passage. The other boats followed Jon's passage technique and continued upstream. It was *Wee Yellow* that did not finish as it wrecked in Grapevine Rapid at river mile eighty-two. Half way up the rapid, the boat plunged nose down into a "hole" and sunk to the bottom of the river. Like the loss of John Wesley Powell's boat the *No Name* in 1869 with its much needed equipment ninety years before, the loss of *Wee Yellow* also meant the loss of all the tools, the fiber glass repair kit, more than 600 unprocessed photographs, and almost a half-mile of movie film.

Ranger Station:
What was the Colorado River like before the completion of Glen Canyon Dam? The flow of the Colorado River was once red, muddy, and voluminous. The construction and 1963 completion of Glen Canyon Dam severely altered the river. After the dam went into full operation, the boulders and cobblestones and sediment and silt that formerly passed through Glen Canyon into Grand Canyon began to settle-out behind the concrete wall of the dam. Unlike the regulated flow of today, the Colorado River once ranged from nearly dry to raging torrent.

Ranger Station:
How do boaters avoid confusion when describing on which side of the Colorado River to run a rapid or make a camp? Facing downstream, the banks of the river are called *river right* and *river left*.

Major John Wesley Powell and Early Expeditions on the Colorado River

Major John Wesley Powell's Colorado River expedition for the purpose of scientific exploration was conceived in 1867 while he was exploring the western waterways in the mountains of Colorado. With the purpose of mapping this frontier of the United States and the territories, the one-armed Major Powell devoted two years in the planning of his river journey. Powell assembled his crew of nine who earned $25 dollars per month with the ability to pan for gold and trap. The trip was taken with great anxiety as the Native American communities told them that the river was wrought with great falls and caverns and were warned "not to try." The expedition began on May 24, 1869, and ended on September 1 of the same year. **The crew** consisted of Powell's brother Walter, William Dunn, William Hawkins, the brothers Oramel and Seneca Howland, John Sumner, George Bradley, Andrew Hall, and Frank Goodman.

Grand Canyoneering: Along with Major John Wesley Powell's equally divided river expedition manifest, the United States War Department permitted him to draw rations at any western fort to provide for his men for ten months. Powell was also able to acquire from the Smithsonian Institution sextants, chronometers (an instrument for measuring time accurately in spite of motion or varying conditions), barometers, thermometers, and compasses. Along with these instruments, Powell obtained abundant clothing, ammunition, hardware such as nails and screws, and assorted tools including axes, hammers, saws, augers, and dozens of traps.

Transportation of Powell's boats and equipment to the frontier West was a critical planning factor. Embarkation coincided with the tie-up of the Union Pacific Railroads' westward track laying schedule with the tracklaying headed eastward by the Central Pacific Railroad. Their "golden spike meeting" at Promontory Point, Utah, on May 10, 1869, was only fourteen days before Powell's departure from Green River, Wyoming.

The boats were built to Powell's specifications by the Bagley Boat Yard of Chicago, Illinois, who constructed four boats, of which one was made of pine and three of double-ribbed, watertight cargo-compartmented oak. These were the *Emma Dean* (which was made of pine), *Kitty Clyde's Sister, Maid of the Canyon,* and the *No Name.* Most noted for the catastrophic end it met in the Ladore Canyon,

Grand Canyoneering: The risks of exploring the western canyon system by boat were encountered long before the one-armed Major John Wesley Powell and his intrepid crew reached the Grand Canyon. Powell's diary entry of June 18, 1869, described the quick-thinking rescue performed by George Young Bradley:

Bradley and I climb [Echo Rock] *until we have ascended 600 or 800 feet when we are met with a sheer precipice. Looking about, we find a place where it seems possible to climb. I go ahead; Bradley follows until we are nearly to the summit. Here, by making a spring, I gain a foothold in a little crevice, and grasp a rock overhead. I find I can get up no farther and cannot step back, for I dare not let go with my hand and cannot reach a foothold below without letting go. I call to Bradley for help. He finds a way to the top of the rock over my head, but cannot reach me. Standing on my toes, my muscles begin to tremble. If I lose my hold I shall fall to the bottom.*

At this instant it occurs to Bradley to take off his long drawers, and he swings them down to me. I hug the rock, seize the dangling legs, and with his assistance gain the top.

located upriver from Grand Canyon, the *No Name* was demolished against the rocks in the Disaster Falls Rapid.

Powell reports in his diary, *The boat strikes a rock, and, rebounding from the shock, careens and fills the open compartment with water. Two of the men lose their oars; she strikes amidships on another rock ... and is broken in two, and the men are thrown into the river; they drift ... to a second rapid, filled with huge boulders, where the boat strikes again and is dashed to pieces. And now the three men are on an island, with a swift, dangerous river on either side, and a fall below. Sumner skillfully plies the oars, and a few strokes set him on the island.*

Frank Goodman resigned on July 5 before the expedition reached Grand Canyon. He informed Powell, *That he has concluded not to go on with the party, saying that he has seen danger enough ... he was one of the crew on the "No Name."* The Grand Canyon had not yet been explored and stagecoach routes circumvented these lands of canyons. On maps to this date, the Grand Canyon was noted as *Terra Incognita*—"earth unknown." Near Marble Canyon, on August 13, Powell writes in his diary, *We are now ready to start our way down the Great Unknown. We have but a month's rations remaining ... an unknown distance yet to run; an unknown river yet to explore. What falls there are we know not.*

The party continues on. Powell writes, *We continue though short of oars. We find a huge pile of driftwood—cottonwood logs—the men set to work sawing oars. Our boats are leaking again. They are turned over, and some of the men are calking them.* After more than 200 river miles into Grand Canyon, with no end in sight and many risks already taken, Oramel Howland informs Powell that he and his brother Seneca and William Dunn have decided not to go any farther. When the men departed the next day, they were given two rifles, and Powell told them to help themselves to what they felt was a fair share of the remaining rations. The trio refused and told Powell that they could survive off the land. Powell writes, *Some tears are shed; it is rather a solemn parting; each party thinks the other is taking the dangerous course.*

The crew members departed the first expedition at an area now known as Separation Canyon. It is popularly thought that Southern Paiute Indians of the North Rim's Shivwits Plateau mistook the members as culprits of their tribe and killed them. Many now think they were victims of the canyon as a route out of Separation Canyon is not probable without climbing gear.

Powell attempted a **second river journey** in 1871–72 due to the loss of important equipment on the first expedition, but did not complete the second trip. Crew member Frederick Dellenbaugh reported, *Powell announced that he decided to end the river work at this point* [Kanab Canyon in Grand Canyon] *on account of the extreme high water, which would render impassable the rapid where the Howlands and Dunn had left.*

Grand Canyoneering: In 1979, Congress approved the Archaeological Resource Protection Act, which defines some site excavation as criminal. With the best intentions, accountability found Frederick Dellenbaugh, crew member of Major John Wesley Powell's 1871–1872 Colorado River expedition, who wrote:

A morning was spent at Tapeats Creek. We found there some ancient house ruins. I discovered a fine large metate and foolishly attempted to take it to camp. On arriving there it was so heavy I had to drop it and it broke in two, much to the Major's disgust, who told me I ought to have let it alone, a fact which I realized then also.

The Howlands and Dunn labyrinthian mystery began on August 28, 1869, when the brothers Seneca and Oramel Howland and William Dunn abandoned Major John Wesley Powell's expedition at Colorado River mile 239.5. Upon reaching the Grand Canyon, the explorers found huge rapids where laborious portaging increased and rations fell drastically short. Now at a time far downstream, and not knowing the journey was nearing the end and fearing the white water of the rapid now aptly named Separation Rapid, morale suffered among the entire crew. The three men attempted to hike out of the canyon against Powell's advice. The trio faced a climb of more than 4,000 feet over unfamiliar terrain in the heat of summer to reach the North Rim region. After the three men departed, the boat *Emma Dean* was abandoned and the main party safely ran the rapid. The fate of the trio is an intriguing mystery. Later, Powell was informed that Southern Paiute Indians of the Shivwits Plateau killed the men near Mount Trumbull, in the area now known as the Arizona Strip. The frontiersmen that went to investigate the incident found no evidence to support the claim against the Paiute Indians. The men

Grand Canyoneering: After the *U.S. Explorer* struck a submerged boulder, Lt. Ives abandoned his vessel. He logged in his journal of March 8, 1858:

We were shooting past Black Canyon when the Explorer, *with a stunning crash, brought up abruptly and instantaneously against a sunken rock. For a second the impression was that the canyon had fallen in. The concussion was so violent that the men near the bow were thrown overboard ... myself, having been seated in the front of the upper deck, (I) precipitated head foremost into the bottom of the boat; the fireman pitching a log into the fire, went half way in with it.*

had no water source or established trail or equipment. In 1997, a team outfitted with climbing gear attempted to retrace the escape route. Their less demanding course, from the rim down, was unsuccessful, suggesting Dunn and the Howlands may have been victims of the canyon.

House Rock Valley is the northeast rim area of Grand Canyon at Marble Canyon. When traveling the area during the second Powell Expedition, crew member Frederick Dellenbaugh noted, *About sunset we passed two large boulders which had fallen together, forming a rude shelter, under which* [Charley] *Riggs or someone else had slept and then had jocosely printed above with charcoal 'Rock House Hotel.' Afterward this served as identification, and House Rock Valley finally went on the maps.*

Music Temple is not in Grand Canyon National Park, but upstream in Glen Canyon. It was held dear by Major John Wesley Powell. Powell wrote in his diary, *Music Temple is a vast chamber. At the upper end is a clear, deep pool. Through the ceiling a thousand feet above there is a narrow winding skylight. Here we bring our camp. When my brother sings us a song at night we are pleased that this hollow is filled with sweet sounds.* Today, the site is under the waters of Lake Powell. Glen Canyon was also named by Powell for its deep beautiful glens—or narrow valleys.

Grand Canyoneering: After the Stanton Survey for an Inner Canyon railroad was underway, rations had fallen drastically short. Splitting up, one team proceeded to Dandy Crossing, Utah, for supplies and the other team continued on with the survey. Stanton's journal recounts the hardship:

One afternoon our cook spied, sitting on a rock, one black crow. Work was stopped ... the whole railroad interest of the country stood still for a while. The cook crept with his Winchester. Our hearts beat quick with joyous expectation. Crack! went the riffle, and behind the rock fell the crow. Into the boat we jumped, and as we floated down the River, our cook grew eloquent on the supper he was going to prepare. We stopped. Just as Gibson went to pick him up, he raised his wings and gracefully flew away ... he had only one leg broken. As that crow soared above us he looked as large as a turkey.

James B. White declared that he ran all of the Colorado River rapids in Grand Canyon two years before Major John Wesley Powell's 1869 expedition. According to White, in the San Juan River Country of the Utah Territory, 500 miles upstream from his point of river exit, Paiute Indians ambushed him and two other prospectors, Charles Baker and George Strole. Baker died in the attack. Abandoning their horses, White and Strole built a raft of cottonwood tree trunks and branches tied together with rope. The pair fled down the river traveling by day and by night. Five days later, the river took Strole's life. Afterward, a rapid destroyed the raft. White built a second raft that became lodged between boulders within the river and could not be freed. A third raft was built while traveling without even the most modest of tools for raft construction and maintenance.

White was rescued at Callville, Nevada Territory, on September 7, 1867. When Robert Brewster Stanton, who knew the river intimately after his railroad surveys beginning in 1889, was asked what he thought of White's claim, he concluded that White must have entered the river below Grand Canyon. Professional river guides agree that covering such a distance from the very rugged San Juan to Callville (now under the waters of Lake Mead) is simply impossible and that White may have entered the river at the Grand Canyon's southwest region of Diamond Creek or Pearce Ferry.

Lieutenant Joseph Christmas Ives and crew were assigned by the United States War Department in 1857 to explore the Colorado River by traveling the river upstream to determine if it could be used to supply western military forts. Ives used the 54-foot long sternwheeler, the *U.S. Explorer*. The ship was built in Philadelphia, Pennsylvania, and tested on the Delaware River. The vessel was then disassembled and shipped to Panama and on to the Pacific Ocean via the Trans-Isthmus Rail Line. Ultimately, the ship was delivered to the Gulf of California for reassembly, tests at sea, and the January 11, 1858, embarkation up the Colorado River. After struggling along the river with trial after trial, the trip ended when the *Explorer* struck a submerged boulder. The lieutenant and some of the crew members set out overland to observe the river en route to eastern Arizona Territory's Fort Defiance. A quote in Ives' 1861 report, *Colorado River of the West*, is ironically made popular by the Grand Canyon visitation of today. Ives informs, *Ours has been the first and doubtless will be the last party ... to visit this profitless locality. It seems intended by nature that the Colorado River shall be forever unvisited and undisturbed.*

Robert Brewster Stanton's Colorado River-Inner Canyon railroad survey is also known as the "Brown Expedition" and the "Stanton Survey." In 1889, the feasibility of building a railroad through the Grand Canyon, with the Colorado River course to serve as the route, was to be determined with a systematic survey by boat. The objective of the railroad was to provide an economical means to ship coal from southern Colorado to California by following the natural terrain to reduce rail construction and to eliminate the importation of coal.

It was S.S. Harper, a northern Arizona prospector, who conceived of a railroad from the Rocky Mountains with a "water grade" via the Colorado River gorge to the Pacific

Jetsam. Robert Brewster Stanton sits in a chair that was found floating down the river during his survey expedition. GRCA 5578

Ocean. Denver engineer John Pierce believed the route entirely practicable. While residing in Denver, Harper became acquainted with a real estate businessman, Frank Brown. Harper discussed a mining venture with Brown. He considered the mining and real estate market over saturated and told Harper that if he could come up with a railroad strategy then he would participate. From this discussion, the Denver, Colorado Canon, and Pacific Railroad was organized.

Frank Brown, as president of the railroad, led the expedition with Robert Stanton in second command. In the planning of the survey, Brown denied the dangers inherent with floating the Colorado River and insisted that no life preservers be taken. Stanton "urged President Brown to provide them [life jackets] for the men. I could make no impression upon Brown." Shortly after the trip began on May 25, 1889, Brown drowned in the Grand Canyon's Marble Canyon at river mile 12 on July 10. On July 15, two crew members, Hansbrough and Richards, also drowned.

Affected by these disasters, the expedition was abandoned on July 18. Stanton led the surviving crew out of the canyon at an area of Marble Canyon, now called Point Retreat, with the promise to return better outfitted. A second expedition assembled on December 10, 1889, close to where the first expedition ended. Stanton completed the survey work, despite great challenges all along the way. Stanton reported, *Compared with other transcontinental railroads ... it would have many advantages ... through the driest section of the western country, have an unlimited supply of water, and it would be possible to operate it by electricity generated by the power of the river tumbling down beside the track.*

Ranger Station:

Did Major John Wesley Powell ever venture away from the confines of the river to view the Grand Canyon from the rims? Major Powell did make investigations of the rims. In 1869, he wrote: "Stand at some point on the brink of the Grand Canyon where you can overlook the river, and the details of the structure, the vast labyrinth of gorges of which it is composed, are scarcely noticed; the elements are lost in the grand effect, and a broad deep flaring gorge of many colors is seen. But stand down among these gorges and the landscape seems to be composed of huge vertical elements of wonderful form."

Ranger Station:

What were Major Powell's achievements after documenting the Colorado River in Grand Canyon? Major Powell established the Smithsonian Institution's Bureau of Ethnology (director until his death in 1902), founded the United States Geological Survey (director 1881–1894), and co-founded the National Geographic Society (1888).

Green River, Wyoming. The start of John Wesley Powell's second expedition. GRCA 14775

Transportation:
Airplanes & Pilots; Automobiles & Roads; Trains; Stagecoaches, Mule Trains & Mules; Bicycles & Skiing

Airplanes & Pilots

Grand Canyoneering: The National Parks Overflights Act was a study first implemented by Superintendent Richard Marks between 1976 and 1981. The Act would empower the Secretary of the Interior to take actions that would protect the environment from the overflight impacts of sight and sound, promoting natural quiet and the reduction of geologically erosive vibration. In 1988, the FAA placed geographical limits on air traffic creating "flight-free" zones based largely on the frequency of above rim and below rim, "blind-spot" midair collisions.

The first airplane to fly over the canyon was on February 24, 1919, by First Lieutenant Ralph Searle and Second Lieutenant E.D. Jones in a DeHavilland DH-4 of the United States Army Air Service.

The first airplane to fly below the canyon rim was on February 25, 1919, by Second Lieutenant Charles Rugh and photographer Lewis Lewyn in a DeHavilland DH-4 of the United States Army Air Service.

The first airplane to land in the canyon was on August 8, 1922, by Royal Thomas and Grand Canyon pioneer and photographer Emery Kolb in a Curtiss Jenny. To form a 300-foot-long airstrip, rangers cleared a path on the Tonto Plateau near Plateau Point.

The first air tour was piloted in 1926 by Charley Mayse in a Lincoln Standard airplane.

Daunting descent. Royal Thomas made the first and only airplane landing on Plateau Point, 1922. GRCA 5255B

Army Air Corps crewmen Roy Embanks, Maurice Cruikshank, and Charles Goldblum parachuted into the canyon from their B-24 Liberator bomber at 12,000 feet on June 20, 1944. The airplane's engines began to shut down in the middle of the night at 28,000 feet and mysteriously restarted at 8,000 feet. The men unwittingly descended into the dark canyon and landed on the remote Tonto

Plateau 4,500 feet below the North Rim and 1,000 feet above the Colorado River. They were supplied by airdrops until aided by ranger Ed Laws and Dr. Alan McRae.

The first helicopter to be used for sightseeing was a Bell 47 piloted by the Hudgin Brothers in 1950. This was the start of the Arizona Helicopter Service.

Grand Canyoneering: In 1926, Parker Van Zandt used a Stinson SM-1 airplane to establish Scenic Airways. Later, Scenic used Ford's Tri Motor "Tin Goose" on the newly constructed, 700 acre Red Butte Airfield located 2 miles east of today's Arizona State Highway 64/U.S. 180. In 1930, Scenic Airways was bought by Jack Thornberg and Ray Schaf for $25,000 and reorganized as *Grand Canyon Airlines*. The operation moved in 1967 to the new Grand Canyon National Park Airport at Tusayan, Arizona, where the Tri Motor was phased out for modern aircraft. Nostalgically, Grand Canyon Airlines brought back the Tri Motor in 1976.

Grand Canyon Airport began service in 1967, 7 aerial miles south of the South Rim. The new airport replaced Red Butte Airfield farther to the south. Grand Canyon Airport can accommodate commercial airliners up to class DC-9 on the 9,000-foot-long paved runway. Historic North Rim landing strips include Tuweep Airstrip, North Rim Airfield, and Lindbergh Hill, which is also known as VT Park for the cattle brand of Van Slack and Thompson. Phoenix's Sky Harbor got its start as an airstrip for tourist flights.

Grand Canyon Airlines hangar. Park personnel and a Travel Air A-600-A airplane at Red Butte Airfield, ca 1934. GRCA 776

Air tours generate approximately $250 million based on an average of 800,000 annual passengers.

Charles Lindbergh landed his airplane at the North Rim Air Field in 1927. Services ended in the 1950s, and a commemorative site, *Lindbergh Hill*, remains at an elevation of 8,960 feet.

Amelia Earhart flew to Grand Canyon in a Lockheed Vega to visit friends at Grand Canyon Airlines in 1935. She then piloted a company airplane for a two-passenger tour.

Hang gliding was evaluated in 1976 to determine the safety and feasibility of glider flight in Grand Canyon National Park. From Maricopa Point, located 1 aerial mile west of the South Rim's El Tovar Hotel at an elevation of 6,900 feet, five pilots came to safe landings on Plateau Point, 3,200 feet below the rim. The activity is not sanctioned by the National Park Service.

A United Airlines and a TWA Airliner catastrophically collided on June 30, 1956, at 21,000 feet over the Colorado and Little Colorado River region in the eastern canyon at the mouth of Marble Canyon. All 128 passengers and crew were killed in the event that occurred 20 aerial miles northeast of the South Rim's El Tovar Hotel. In the original flight plan, there was to be a take off separation of 34 minutes. However, a maintenance delay on the TWA Super Constellation airliner reduced the separation to three minutes. An hour-and-a-half after take off, at 10:31 a.m., Aeronautical Radio agents in San Francisco, California, and Salt Lake City, Utah, heard voices transmitting from the United Airlines DC-7, *Up! ... Up! ... Salt Lake, United 718 ... ah ... we're going in.*

Grand Canyoneering: Papillon Grand Canyon Helicopters was established in 1965 by Elling Halvorson. While building the Trans-Canyon Water Line, he used helicopters to ferry construction materials to the work sites. During one such flight, the idea was conceived to offer sightseeing flights around and in Grand Canyon National Park.

Severe disintegration and fire followed impact with the canyon. The collision went into the canyon noses first, and the wreckage was distributed on the area of Temple and Chuar Buttes. Interior materials from the TWA flight were found on the southeast canyon rim at Cape Solitude, 2 miles to the east, indicating that they were separated from the plane at a sufficient altitude to drift that distance. On the pieces that survived the intense impact, collision evidence was found in the form of dents and scratches, and black deicer boot and paint smudges.

In the Civil Aeronautics Board's investigation, the conclusion was made that clouds from a storm at 21,000 feet could have obscured the pilots' vision and that

Grand Canyoneering: A railroad was outlined in 1909 to determine the feasibility of constructing a line from southern Utah to the North Rim. The objectives of such a railroad included the harvest of the Kaibab Plateau's old growth forests and to promote tourism by providing convenient and scenic wilderness access. Still, visitation was sparse in the years of Theodore Roosevelt's trip to the very remote and rugged North Rim. The extreme grade right-of-way from Fredonia, Arizona, at the Utah border, to the rim and the lack of the ability to travel to the railhead region were key factors in dooming support for a railway system.

Meanwhile, in those tranquil years, regional lumbering remained small-scale and portable. Operated by Levi Stewart's Big Spring Ranch, the first sawmill was most likely the steam-powered device that was brought in from Skutumpah, Utah, in 1871. Almost eighty years later, in 1950, pioneering lumbering efforts made the transition to the large-scale Kaibab Lumber Company in Fredonia to process the timber harvests that were carried out on the Kaibab Plateau.

the planes may have been flown so that each plane was on either side of the cloud build-up. The Civil Aeronautics Board also concluded that the collision could have been the result of limited cockpit visibility, preoccupation with normal duties or unrelated duties, such as attempting to improve passenger view of the Grand Canyon. Memorial monuments are at the Grand Canyon Pioneer Cemetery on the South Rim and at The Citizens Cemetery at Flagstaff, Arizona. Today, backcountry hikers continue to encounter pieces of the wreckage. Because of this, the worst disaster in aviation history up to that date, the Federal Government created the Federal Aviation Administration.

Logs and shake shingles. South Rim Standard Oil gas station at Desert View, 1939. GRCA 844

Automobiles & Roads

The first car to reach the South Rim was on January 2, 1902, and was driven by Oliver Lippencott, who was guided by Al Doyle. The passengers were Thomas Chapman and journalist Winfield Hogaboom. The vehicle was a steam-powered American Bicycle Company Model C Toledo Eight-horse. The trip originated out of Flagstaff, Arizona, where shortly afterwards the car broke down. After repairs, the car ran out of gas eighteen miles short of the rim. Hogaboom walked to the South Rim at the Grand View area to find help and found Peter Berry, who retrieved the other men. Berry then went to the railroad to get gasoline. It took five days to get the vehicle to the South Rim, but only seven hours to return to Flagstaff.

The first cars to reach the North Rim were in June 1909. Driving the steep grade out of Kanab, Utah, the trip took three days in a Thomas Flyer and a Locomobile. To ensure a timely arrival, gasoline was staged along the way.

The first car to reach the Colorado River was in 1912, and was driven by Byron Graves of the Ford Motor Company. When the car reached the river at Diamond Creek, it was promoted as America's most durable vehicle.

Fueling station. The "Oil House," North Rim, 1949. GRCA 1775

The Hermit Road is the historic **Hermit Rim Road** that was for a time called the **West Rim Drive.** From 1910 to 1912, at the cost of $180,000, the Santa Fe Railroad constructed the road utilizing a 30-foot-wide roadbed that was covered with crushed stone. Once used by stagecoaches, the road provided tourist access to the toll-free Hermit Trail owned by the Santa Fe Railroad. Designed in 1914 by Mary Colter, Hermits Rest followed. This diverted tourists away from the then Bright Angel Toll Trail owned by Ralph Cameron and, eventually, by Coconino County. Access is located immediately west of the Bright Angel Trail and transportation is conducted by automobile during the winter and shuttle bus during the summer. The 8-mile-long two-lane roadway is composed of a light duty pavement and consists of 5 named sections: El Tovar Hill, Coconino Wash, Tusayan Hill, Hopi Wall, and Cataract Canyon Country. El Tovar Hill provides a view of Grand Canyon Village and El Tovar Hotel on the return drives' 112-foot descent of the Bright Angel Fault. Cataract Canyon Country provides distant views of the Cataract-Havasu Canyon region.

Grand Canyoneering: Roads in Grand Canyon National Park were unpaved prior to 1930.

Rowe Well Road, named for pioneer Sanford Rowe, is partially paved and intersects the historic Hermit Road at its beginning, west of the Bright Angel Trail. Traveling south, Rowe Well Road extends outside Grand Canyon National Park and continues for 5 miles into the Kaibab National Forest. Rowe Well Road junctions with the westerly Forest Service Road 605 which accesses the outlying Havasupai Indian Reservation, the South Bass Trail, and the site of the historic Bass Camp.

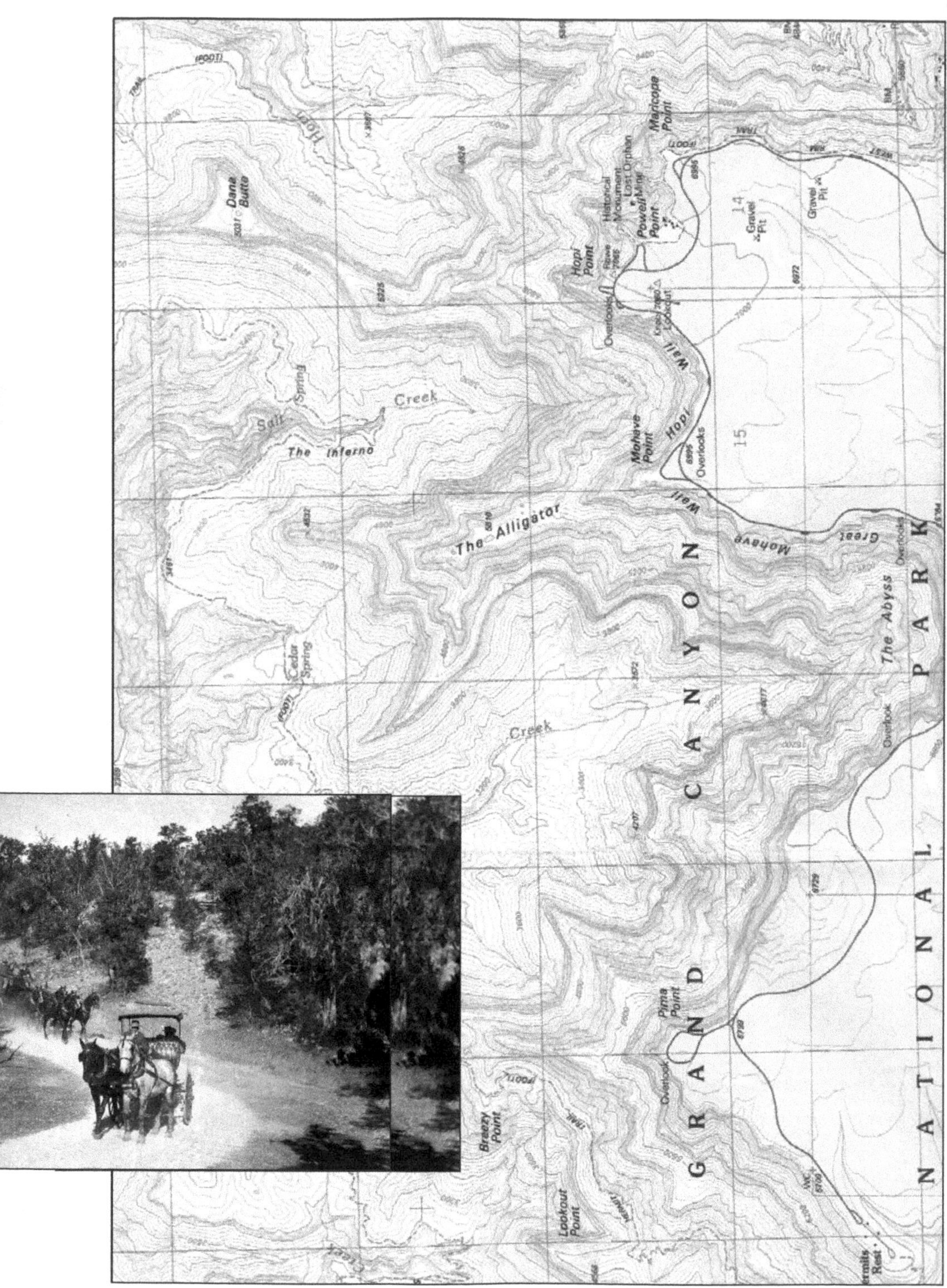

Hermit Rim Road, South Rim. USGS 7.5 minute series *Grand Canyon*
Inset: **The Hermit Rim Road, 1911.** Stagecoaching the South Rim on the "new road" eight years before the establishment of Grand Canyon National Park. USDA, Forest Service

The Desert View–East Rim Drive is a 25-mile-long, two-lane medium-light duty paved roadway that is a section of Arizona State Highway 64. This section is known today as Desert View Drive. South of the South Rim, the horse-drawn wagon tracks in Long Jim Canyon were used prior to 1958 as a partial route to Grand Canyon Village. Access points include Yaki Point, which provides access to the South Kaibab Trail; Grand View Point, site of the Grand View Trail; the Arizona Trail; Shoshone Point; Moran Point; Tusayan Ruin; Lipan Point; Navajo Point; Desert View, which is the site of the East Entrance Station; and the Indian Watchtower.

The Cape Royal Road of the North Rim is a 21-mile-long road that was constructed between 1927 and 1929. From its beginning at the junction with the entrance highway, the Cape Royal Road travels through Fuller Canyon to the road fork at Neal Spring and the head of Bright Angel Creek. This road section, called the **Point Imperial Road,** travels northeastward for three miles to its cul-de-sac at Point Imperial—the highest North Rim overlook, at an elevation of 8,803 feet. Back at Neal Spring the road travels southeast to where the traveler encounters dramatic overlooks including Vista Encantada (also referred to as Vista Encantadora), elevation 8,480 feet; the unimproved Cape Final, elevation 7,916 feet, where there is a 1.7-mile long trail out to the rim and a view of Juno Temple; the Walhalla Overlook, at an elevation of 7,994 feet, which provides the broadside view of Angels Window; and Cape Royal, elevation 7,865 feet, where there are commanding views of Wotans Throne, Vishnu Temple, and the far distances to and beyond the South Rim. From these North Rim vantage points, one can see 80 to 100 miles with the naked eye.

Grand Canyoneering: The Grand Canyon National Park support town of Tusayan, Arizona, is located outside the park 6 aerial miles south of the South Rim's El Tovar Hotel. The community is capped by the South Rim Entrance Station to the north and the Grand Canyon National Park Airport to the south. The town, bisected by Highways 64/180, is a portion of a 160-acre homestead purchased for $20,000 in the 1930s by Bob Thurston.

Arizona State Highway 67 from Jacob Lake, Arizona, to the North Rim Entrance Station is termed the **Kaibab Plateau North Rim Parkway.** The original United States Forest Service–administered Grand Canyon Highway was constructed in 1913. The 13-mile-long entrance highway extending from the log entrance station to Grand Canyon Lodge, which is still in use today, was realigned in 1930.

Trains

The railroad to the South Rim arose from the need to transport ore from the Grand Canyon area Anita Copper Mines to Williams, Arizona. In 1899, the firm of Lombard, Goode, and Company raised the capital that started the Canyon Construction Company. On March 15, 1900, the tracks reached the Anita Mines, 45 miles north of Williams and 20 miles short of the South Rim. The tracks were, however, in-line with the Cameron Trail, which today is known as the Bright Angel Trail, and Grand Canyon Village. Later, the railroad was reorganized as the Grand Canyon Line, a subsidiary of the Santa Fe Railroad. The tracks were extended to the South Rim when tourism steadily increased through the efforts of the stagecoach lines originating from Flagstaff, Arizona. Train travel replaced the stagecoach travel industry when on September 1, 1901, the first passenger train arrived at Grand Canyon's South Rim.

As automobiles became the chief means of transportation, the last train run was on July 30, 1968. Twenty years later in 1988, Max and Thelma Biegert reorganized the line as the Grand Canyon Railway. In an effort to reduce automobile traffic in the village area, the National Park Service welcomed the first train back from the 1908 built Williams, Arizona, Fray Marcos Depot, which arrived at the South Rim on September 17, 1989. Today, the Grand Canyon Railway is operated by Xanterra Parks and Resorts.

Glory restored. Grand Canyon Railway's #18 at Grand Canyon Depot. GRCA

Top: **Off the rails at Tooker's Cut.** Atchison, Topeka and Santa Fe's Engine #3853 south of Grand Canyon Village, Coconino Wash, 1939. GRCA 696

Right: **Derailed.** Train cars followed Atchison, Topeka and Santa Fe's Engine #3853 at Tooker's Cut, 1939. GRCA 698

The Apex, Arizona, historic site is located 4 aerial miles south of the South Rim and was built in 1901 as a siding for passing trains en route to the rim at the Anita-Apex summit. In 1893, the Saginaw Lumber Company obtained timber licensing and built spur lines eastward through today's Kaibab National Forest. After a merger with the Manistee Lumber Company, they became the primary lumber contractor to Grand Canyon Village during the lodge construction era.

Stagecoaches, Mule Trains & Mules

Mule trains, running commercially on the Bright Angel Trail, are thought to have been run first by pioneer Martin Buggeln. **Mules** are three times stronger than horses and twice as agile. Smoother to ride than a horse, mules posses an intelligence many believe superior to that of the horse. Before carrying passengers, canyon mules receive extensive training and evaluation for obedience and discipline. To reduce the risk of injury to the animal, Grand Canyon mules are fitted with a custom bridle and saddle. Marked as the safest year-round trail ride in the world, mules are fitted with a "snow shoe" for winter travel. The winter mule shoe is fashioned with tungsten carbide "chips" on the ground contact surface to keep the mules from slipping on icy trails. Once selected for Inner Canyon travel, mules make up to six round-trips per week. Most of the mules selected for the Grand Canyon are stock chosen from Missouri and Tennessee. Rider qualifications include a minimum height of 4 feet 7 inches and a body weight of less than 200 pounds.

> **Grand Canyoneering:** Fred Harvey Company Trail Boss, John Bradley, related this humorous story about his Grand Canyon mules. The quip begins with a timid question from the first time rider (or dude):
> **Dude:** Have you a real gentle mule for me?
> **Wrangler:** *No ma'am, I'm right sorry, but we just sent the last gentle mule down the trail with the last party. If you ain't ever rode before, why we'll just have to give you a mule that ain't ever been rode before either, an' you can start out right together!*

Riparian paddock. Mule shelter and corral at the Colorado River and Bright Angel Creek, 1935. GRCA 896

Historical stagecoach route maps clearly illustrate that the Grand Canyon was avoided. Not yet the popular tourist destination that it is today, the canyon system posed an extreme barrier to travelers before the late 1800s. At the time, stagecoaches to the South Rim became the normal transportation mode for the new-found Grand Canyon tourist trade, but would last only until the arrival of train travel in 1901. Stagecoaches transported the majority of tourists using four and six horse rigs. These rough rides competed and originated from Ash Fork, Williams, and Flagstaff, Arizona. The run from Flagstaff required the services of Hull (East Cedar Ranch), Dillman, Moqui, and Red Horse (photo page 130) relay stations for a change of horses and occasional overnight stays. These stations were located in general alignment with Flagstaff and the South Rim near Grand View Point, 10 aerial miles southeast of today's Grand Canyon Village. Stagecoaches were operated by a host of Grand Canyon pioneers such as William Bass and partners John Hance and the Hull Brothers. But it was James Thurber who customized and consistently upgraded the journeys with state-of-the-art coaches and services beginning in 1895. When the railroad came within 10 miles of the South Rim, Thurber reacted by building the Bright Angel Hotel, the predecessor to the Bright Angel Lodge, in 1896. He then ran his coaches from "end-of-track" to his hotel. The **North Rim** saw stagecoach service offered by E.D. Wooley and his son-in-law, David Rust, who provided service from Kanab, Utah, to the sparsely visited high country in 1907.

Landmark steeple. The Fred Harvey Mule Barn and its spired vent cupola, South Rim, 1997. GRCA 18274

Grand Canyoneering: James Thurber was essential with regard to transporting the Grand Canyon tourist. As the train and automobile advanced the tourist in quantity and comfort in the years following Thurber, he implemented the next logical step from the single horse and rider or buckboard.

In 1894, Thurber purchased the Flagstaff, Arizona, based horse facilities of William Dickerson to further compete in the endeavor of tourist conveyance. Along with his concurrently owned Bright Angel Hotel from 1896 to 1901, Thurber operated the Grand Canyon Stage Line from Flagstaff to the South Rim at Hance Camp, 12 aerial miles east of the budding Grand Canyon Village. Thurber had incisive business discernment and the means to upgrade the coaches. As innovations occurred, he kept up with the rising expectations of the tourist.

When the railroad approached the South Rim at mining interest Anita Junction, Thurber's business immediately withered. He responded by developing the Bright Angel Stage Line. This stagecoach shuttle ran from the "end-of-track" at Anita to his Bright Angel Hotel on the South Rim—a rustic 10-mile journey through the pine forest.

The Bright Angel Stage Line was created by James Thurber when the Grand Canyon Railway was established from Williams, Arizona, to the South Rim region at a designation called Anita. His stage line ran from "end-of-track" to the Bright Angel Hotel, the predecessor to the Bright Angel Lodge.

Ranger Station:

How did stagecoach operators move such a large number of tourists from the railroad at Flagstaff, Arizona, to the canyon's South Rim? Six-horse double stagecoach rigs were used, sometimes called a set or a tandem. Before the advent of pulling doubles, the simple answer was to have tourists ride on the roofs of the stagecoaches.

Ranger Station:

Whose idea was it to bring Apollo program astronauts to the Grand Canyon to learn geology? In March 1964, USGS geologist Dale Jackson first took the astronauts to the Grand Canyon, where memorable outcrops illustrate basic stratigraphic principals "better than any classroom."

Ranger Station:

Where do the mules for the Grand Canyon come from, and who chooses the mules? What is expected of hikers who encounter a mule string on the trail?Usually chosen from the states of Tennessee and Missouri, mule stock is typically selected for travel in the Grand Canyon by the trail boss. Mules are first employed to pack supplies to Phantom Ranch and pack mail and goods out of the canyon. During this time of "apprenticeship," rookie Grand Canyon mules are assessed for overall disposition prior to their promotion to passenger transportation.

For the safety of everyone on the Bright Angel, River, and Kaibab Trails, where mules travel, hikers encountering a string of mules must stop to one side of the trail. Out of the way of the mules, stand quietly to avoid contacting or startling a mule. Listen for and respect the instructions of the wrangler. Wait until the mule string has passed.

Bicycles & Skiing

The Coconino Cycling Club was a group that accepted a dare to ride the 70-mile-long stagecoach route from Flagstaff, Arizona, starting in 1894. The bikes typical of the day could not withstand the rugged stage route and would mechanically fail. Downed riders would wait for stagecoach transportation to the South Rim in the monsoons of August. Because the trip was an overwhelming challenge, the event continued only until 1897.

Skiing cross-country style is possible on the North Rim due to the accumulation of snow that ranges from 120 to 200 inches per year. **The North Timp Point Snowmobile Route** utilizes a dozen United States Forest Service roads in the Kaibab National Forest, adjacent to the North Rim, to create an 80-mile round trip course from Jacob Lake, Arizona, where much of the route is above 8,000 feet in elevation.

Grand Canyoneering: Many Apollo astronauts, including Neil Armstrong and Jim Lovell, have spent time at the Grand Canyon. Beginning in 1964, the astronauts studied the Grand Canyon's geology with naturalist Edwin McKee to gain a better understanding of lunar specimen collection and identification. After stepping onto the Earth's moon, Armstrong said, *It's a very soft surface, but here and there a very hard surface. It has a stark beauty like much of the high desert of the United States.*

Native Americans and Ruins

Ancestral Puebloans, formerly called the Anasazi Indians, inhabited the Grand Canyon area from approximately 900–1200 A.D. These Native American Southwest beginnings are recognized as starting in 1 A.D. Ancestral Puebloans is now the term applied to the predecessors of the Hopi Indians and other Native American groups. *Anasazi* has various interpretations including, "ancient ones," "ancient enemies," and "enemy ancestors." Ancestral Puebloans were hunters, gatherers, and agriculturists who lived on the rims and in the canyon. There are as many as 2,500 known archaeological sites. Archaeologists agree that many more undiscovered sites remain undisturbed due to remoteness and camouflaging.

Grand Canyoneering: Native American Grand Canyon creation legends include, from the South Rim's **Havasupai**: *Hokomata,* the evil god of the universe, who quarreled with his righteous brother Tochopa and decided to drown the world. The good brother put his daughter in a hollow log for safety. The floods came, covering the world, and the swirling waters carved Chicamimi—*Grand Canyon.* From the South Rim's **Hualapai**: After a flood covered the earth, *Packithaawi,* the hero god, came with his magic knife. He cleaved the canyon and the water receded through the fissure forming the river. From the North Rim's **Paiute**: A great chief mourned the death of his wife, Numa, and found no comfort until the Paiute god, *Tavwoats* took him to see her. Tavwoats made a trail, the canyon, through a mountain range. He created a river, the Colorado, as he led Numa's husband along the trail. Finding Numa happy, the chief returned to the world.

Window to a past culture. Pueblo pottery excavated in Tusayan Ruin, 1930. GRCA 3130

What happened to the tribe? During a time called "The Abandonment," the Ancestral Puebloan possibly departed the region due to a 23-year-long drought. The shortage of water is known based on area tree ring studies (dendrochronology), having occurred circa 1276–1299. In addition, the tribes spent summers on the cooler rims and wintered in the warmer Inner Canyon. Introduced here, it is possible that massive flooding of the Colorado River System, as indicated by prehistoric driftwood lodged in high cliff caves and atop monolithic boulders in the river, accentuated by heavy rains supercharged by the melting snow from the North and South Rims during an unseasonable winter hot spell, may have further influenced tribal populations.

The Havasupai Indians (Havasu 'Baaja) are the ancestors of the Cerbat Indians who moved north from the lower Colorado River region. The tribe added agriculture to a hunting and gathering lifestyle. *Havasupai* means "people of the blue-green water."

> **Grand Canyoneering:** In 1910, a hot spell in January followed months of snowfall. In the sudden melting of snow, the Coconino Plateau's Grand Canyon rim drainage and underground channels swelled. The water overwhelmed the head of Havasu Canyon and rushed downstream and destroyed the Havasupai Indian Village of Supai—which is restored after each flood.

The village of the Havasupai, called "Supai," is located 33 aerial miles northwest of the South Rim's El Tovar Hotel at an elevation of 3,195 feet, 7 miles upstream from the confluence of Havasu Creek and the Colorado River. In 1880, President Rutherford B. Hayes prompted the establishment of the Havasupai Indian Reservation. Approval arrived under President Chester A. Arthur and Havasupai Chief Navajo. In 1975, a 185,000-acre land reinstatement was congressionally authorized and approved by President Gerald R. Ford. The main access to Supai is near Peach Springs, Arizona, via the 60-mile-long paved Indian Route 18, which is a northerly light-duty road off U.S. Route 66. The trailhead is located at the end of Indian Route 18 at a parking lot at Hualapai Hilltop, elevation 5,199 feet. The trail is 8 miles long from the rim of the canyon to Supai. Called the Ladder, the trail switchbacks for 1.5 miles until it reaches the seasonally dry creek bed of Hualapai Canyon. The trail continues to Havasu Canyon and the village, populated by 600 people. Use of other access routes, such as the extremely remote and rugged Topocoba Trail through Lee Canyon, are by the exclusive permission of the Havasupai.

One room. Schoolhouse at Havasupai, 1939. GRCA 179

The Hopi Sipapu, pronounced *see-paw-poo,* is a spring-formed calcium carbonate dome in the Little Colorado River region. Hopi legend says that the Sipapu is where the forefathers of the human race emerged from the underworld. Within the opening of the formation are slender twigs with attached feathers called prayer

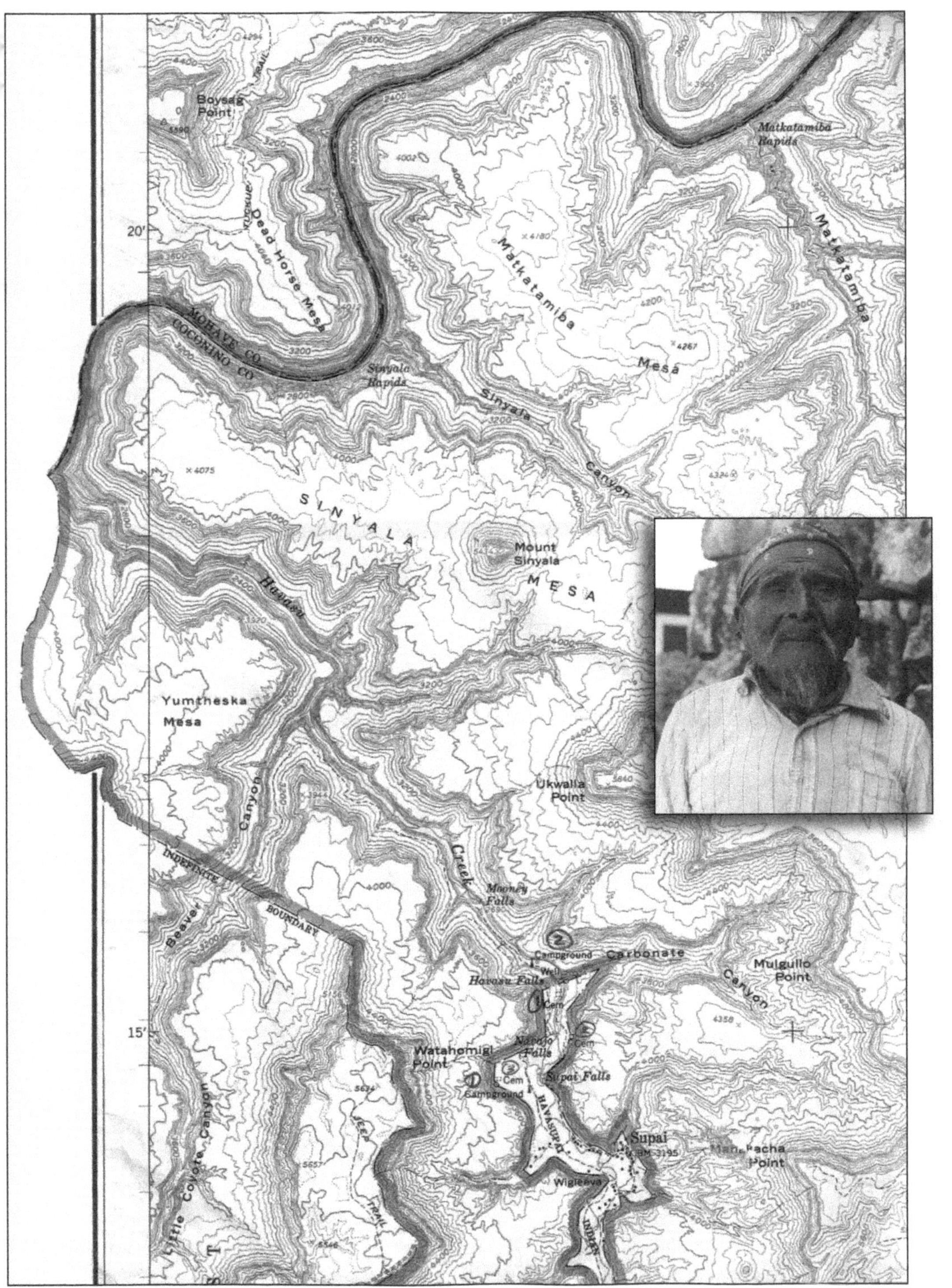

Above: Supai, Arizona, Inner Canyon. USGS *Grand Canyon National Park and Vicinity*
Inset: **Yavñmi Gswedva, which means "Dangling Beard" (1856–1952).** Prominent Havasupai tribal leader who was called "Big Jim," 1947. GRCA 987

sticks. The Sipapu inspired the form of the ceremonial kiva. Inside the kiva, typically in the north-facing wall, is a 6-inch deep pocket symbolic of the Sipapu.

The Hualapai Indians, *Hualupai* meaning "people of the pines," are of the Cohonina and Yuman Indians. The Hualapai Indian Reservation, located on the southwest rim area, was established by President Chester A. Arthur. The Hualapai Indian's **Skywalk at Grand Canyon West** is a U-shaped steel platform that extends 70-feet from the South Rim at Eagle Point and is cantilevered 4,000 feet above the canyon floor. The Skywalk was designed by architect David Jin and built by Lochsa Engineering at the cost of $30 million. The inaugural walk event on the multilayered glass floor was on March 20, 2007, with guests of honor, astronauts John Bennett Herrington and Buzz Aldrin.

Grand Canyoneering: The Wigleeva are two side-by-side rock spires positioned on the canyon rim above and west of the village of Supai. The formation is interpreted as the petrified remains of two brothers who led the Havasupai tribe to safety and perpetuated tribal existence, provided The Wigleeva remain in place. West of Grand Canyon National Park, but adjoining the southwest park boundary, is the Havasupai Indian Reservation.

The Navajo Indian Reservation was established in 1868 with 3,500,000 acres and later increased to 16,000,000 acres. The *Diné Bikéyah*, or "Navajoland," adjoins the Grand Canyon National Park boundaries at the southerly Marble Canyon and Grand Canyon's easterly Main Corridor. Both areas are bisected by the Little Colorado River. *Diné* means "The People."

The Nankoweap Ruin, located 13 aerial miles northeast of the North Rim's Grand Canyon Lodge at an elevation of 3,300 feet, is a remote Inner Canyon Native American feature. Ancestral Puebloans, once called Anasazi, constructed the granary approximately 500 feet above the Colorado River under the overhanging cliffs of Nankoweap Mesa. There are four primary entry points and a fifth opening termed a "porthole." *Nankoweap* is the Paiute Indian word meaning, "canyon of echos."

Mallery Grotto, located below the South Rim, is in the vicinity of El Tovar Hotel. The exact location is not revealed here to preserve site integrity. The alcove is named for Native American pictograph authority, Garrick Mallery. The pictograph setting represents sheep, deer, and humans.

Shaman's Gallery is the Native American religious and ceremonial foregathering place that includes life-size multicolored pictographs of birds, animals, and humans. The location is not revealed here to preserve site integrity.

Where eagles pass. Nankoweap Ruin opposite the "East Rim" at Blue Moon Bench. GRCA D3516

Cibola is the collective name given to the seven Zuni Indian pueblos in present-day northwest New Mexico, which inspired Spanish exploration to the Grand Canyon region in 1540.

Ancient footpaths. Tusayan Ruin, South Rim. GRCA

The Tusayan Ruins are located 15 aerial miles east of the South Rim's El Tovar Hotel. The stabilized ruin site is accessed by traveling the Desert View–East Rim Drive east for 23 miles from Mather Point. Tusayan, pronounced *too-say-on*, is from the Zuni word for the Hopi-Oraibi settlement of Usayakye. The word was mispronounced by the Spanish during their regional exploration in the 1500s. Directed by Harold S. Gladwin, the staff of the Gila Pueblo at Globe, Arizona, excavated the ruin in 1930. Because trees were used in the roof construction of the Ancestral Puebloan community, the settlement was dated 1185 A.D. using tree ring studies (dendrochronology).

The site was populated for approximately 25 years by some thirty people. This was determined by studying pottery styles, measuring wear on cornmeal grinding stones, and scrutinizing rubbish that was left in some of the smaller "compartments." The rubbish also helped to define their lifestyle. There are five living quarters in the fifteen-room, two kiva, structure. The pueblo had no formal doors and no windows. An opening over each room provided access. The lack of openings provided warmth, but certainly did not effectively vent the smoke emitted from interior fire pits. Respiratory complications must have been inevitable. The courtyard faces south to utilize the sun in the winter and to acknowledge the tribally-sacred **San Francisco Peaks.** In addition to growing beans, corn, and squash, the group also gathered and hunted. The MacCurdy-Tusayan Museum was constructed in 1932.

Grand Canyoneering: Built in 1908, the Hopi Fire Tower is located on the South Rim, along the Hermit Road near Hopi Point, at an elevation of 7,140 feet. The tower required reconstruction in 1913 and 1954 due to lightning strikes. The funds to rehabilitate the tower in 1954 were acquired by Superintendent Harold C. Bryant who requisitioned $150 to replace the floor and roof.

Today, in addition to observation, the tower is used to monitor the air quality at Grand Canyon. At the height of just 23 feet 6 inches, the structure is much shorter than a common tower, as less prominence is required to see over the shorter pinyon pine and juniper trees of the Kaibab Forest.

Walhalla Glades Ruin is located 8 aerial miles southeast of the North Rim's Grand Canyon Lodge at an elevation of 7,994 feet on the Walhalla Plateau. *Glades* is Anglo-Saxon for "glad," referring to "bright and sunny." It is thought that this site was occupied by the Ancestral Puebloan, once called Anasazi, between 1050 and 1150 A.D. Only a rock outline remains of the nine-room structure made of the Kaibab Limestone Formation that once stood in Walhalla Glades. Adobe and timber used in ceiling construction suggest that the entrance would have been by ladder through an opening over each room similar to the South Rim's Tusayan site. Interior fire pits were used for heat and cooking for some fifteen to twenty-five people who occupied the dwelling on this sky island. A granary is found along the Cliff Spring Trail. It was used for the beans, corn, and squash that were grown at more than 100 locations. It is possible that the Ancestral Puebloans moved seasonally from this site to the Inner Canyon at Unkar Creek and Delta, at Colorado River mile 73, where there are more ruin sites.

Bright Angel Pueblo is located in the canyon, 7 aerial miles southwest of the North Rim's Grand Canyon Lodge near the mouth of Bright Angel Creek at the Colorado River. The site was excavated and assessed in 1969 by Douglas Schwartz of the American School of Research and is now a stabilized ruin. Perhaps as many as sixteen people lived here in the four rooms beginning in 1050 A.D. In a period called "the Abandonment," desertion followed 90 years later in 1140 A.D. for reasons that may include drought. A ceremonial kiva is located between the river and the dwelling site.

Photo by Flood Hefley

In Hualapai Canyon. From the village of Supai near the bottom of the canyon, horses belonging to the Havasupai travel the eight miles to the South Rim at Hualapai Hilltop—alone.

Ranger Station:

Where did the name Anasazi come from and why the name change to Ancestral Puebloan? The term Anasazi was first used by rancher Richard Wetherill of Mancos, Colorado, to refer to the early people of plateaus, mesas, buttes, and canyons. Through contact with the Navajo (Diné), the Wetherill family understood their word anaasa'zi, or "enemy ancesters," which refers to the Ancestral Puebloan (also called Ancestral Puebloans and Ancestral Pueblo). The name was assigned and the spelling abridged to Anasazi. Later, the people group included those who occupied the Grand Canyon.

The name Anasazi was changed in recent times to recognize that being defined as "enemy ancesters" is belittling to some tribes. Since the Hopi at no time call anyone enemy, the term is particularly offensive to this people group, who claim direct lineage. Since there are several Pueblo languages, archaeologists termed the people Ancestral Puebloan.

Ranger Station:

What materials did the ancient inhabitants of the Grand Canyon area use for construction? The Tusayan Ruin site on the South Rim is an amazing piece of architecture considering the Ancestral Puebloan had limited resources.

Pinyon pine was used in pueblo rafter construction and as firewood for warmth and meal preparation (the pinyon pine seed, or "nut," was also a staple food item). The Colorado pinyon, dominant in the Grand Canyon woodlands of the South Rim, was used primarily. The tree is also found on the North Rim at elevations of 7,700' and below and at Inner Canyon elevations of 4,000' and above.

The Utah juniper served as fuel. Fiber work in sandals and insulation also utilized the shredded bark, and food or seasoning was made from the pine cone, or berry.

Pioneers and Historic Buildings

The Grand Canyon Pioneer Cemetery, located west of the National Park Headquarters, currently holds 305 plots. Interred are those closely associated with Grand Canyon National Park. The interment of pioneer John Hance among a few unmarked graves defined formal cemetery commencement.

Grand Canyoneering: In the early 1900s, William Ashurst, a prospector and trail builder, died in a rockslide .5 mile upstream on the Colorado River from Bright Angel Canyon. A slab of Vishnu Schist Formation rock fell on Ashurst and pinned him to the ground. He was found 49 days later as determined by his last journal entry. Niles Cameron retrieved his remains and buried them at the head of the Bright Angel Trail. Circa 1934, the National Park Service transferred and interred Ashurst in the Grand Canyon National Park Cemetery.

Emma Ayer toured the Grand Canyon in 1885 with husband Edward, who owned a Flagstaff, Arizona, based sawmill. Mrs. Ayer was the first female Caucasian documented to have hiked to the Colorado River. She followed the precipitous Hance Trail to the river with guide John Hance.

Quiet contemplation. William Bass, ca 1910. GRCA 3635

William Wallace Bass was born in Shelbyville, Indiana, and moved west seeking improved health. Bass lived 60 years beyond his doctor's expectation—only dying in 1933 at the age of 83. After his arrival in 1884, Bass brought the Grand Canyon to the attention of the American people. He developed the trans-canyon North and South Bass Trails, which were aided by his cable crossing. With his Grand Canyon career well underway, Bass married New England Conservatory of Music graduate Ada Diefendorf. While raising her family (the Basses had four children), Ada regularly traveled from the South Rim to the Colorado River to accomplish the task of doing laundry.

Peter D. Berry arrived at the South Rim in 1890 after attending to his brother, who was shot in a barroom brawl in Flagstaff, Arizona. Peter Berry hoped for rich mineral strikes and joined other prospectors, such as Ralph Cameron, in developing the Bright Angel Trail. The team hurriedly staked copper claims on Horseshoe Mesa, located below Grand View Point, 9 aerial miles east of the South Rim's El Tovar Hotel. When mining proved inefficient and too expensive to operate, Berry focused on tourism by building the Grand View Hotel. By 1913, Berry sold his property to William Randolph Hearst, who in turn sold most of the property to the National Park Service in 1941. The Hearst Corporation today owns a 450-acre Inner Canyon in-holding.

Grand Canyoneering: Commencement for the United States Post Office at Grand Canyon was at Hance Camp, east of Grand Canyon Village. From 1894–1897, the office was designated as Tollfree, Arizona. Three months after closing, the post office re-opened and was designated Tourist, Arizona, and John Hance was appointed Postmaster.

Louis Boucher of the Boucher and Dripping Springs Trails is popularly credited with lending the "Hermit" name to the area of the South Rim that is 8 aerial miles west of Grand Canyon Village. Louis Boucher largely led a hermit's lifestyle, though associating with many tourists. Historian and western author George Wharton James credits Louis P. Brown with the designation of Hermit Basin, located immediately below Hermits Rest.

Buffalo Bill (William Frederick Cody) arrived at the South Rim in November 1892 with an entourage of British sportsmen. The party ventured onward and used Lees Ferry at the head of Marble Canyon to cross the Colorado River to the North Rim for a mountain lion hunt. Sponsored by the son of Brigham Young, the hunt was an effort of John Young to build the Utah tourist trade by promoting the Kaibab Plateau as a hunter's destination.

Martin Buggeln was one of the first pioneers to recognize Grand Canyon for its tourist trade potential. Buggeln owned the Grand Canyon Hotel in Williams, Arizona, 60 miles south of the South Rim before acquiring the Bright Angel Hotel in 1901. It is thought that Martin Buggeln ran the first commercial mule-back transportation service on the Bright Angel Trail, and then turned the business over to the Fred Harvey Company in 1904. Buggeln anticipated wealth with the coming of the Santa Fe Railroad. However, the railroad built the El Tovar Hotel, which created a division in the tourist market share. In 1905, Buggeln sold his interests and in 1906 purchased the John Hance property and the Hance Hotel. When this project failed, Buggeln sold again and left the area. Today, a picnic area located on the Desert View–East Rim Drive's north shoulder commemorates Martin Buggeln with Buggeln Hill.

Ralph Henry Cameron arrived at the South Rim in 1883 and led the area in filing mining claims. To access many of the claims, Cameron improved Inner Canyon routes, including the Bright Angel Trail. Soon after setting up for mining, he recognized that mining would give way to tourism. In an effort to control as much land as possible, Cameron took advantage of federal mining claim enactments and filed more than 100 claims. By doing this, he was able to retain much of the South Rim and Inner Canyon property. Cameron operated the Bright Angel Toll Trail until he was defeated in legal conflicts.

Grand Canyoneering: For 11 years, from 1883–1894, John Hance led tourists into the canyon on the Hance Trail, which was a Havasupai Indian trail that Hance improved. The trail descended to Hance Creek, below the east arm of Horseshoe Mesa. This trail fell into disuse when the route was obliterated by rock slides. After these rock slides in 1894, Hance rerouted the trail through Red Canyon east of the original trail. Over 100 years old, the New Hance Trail is still in use by the most experienced of Grand Canyon backpackers descending to the Colorado River at the Hance Rapid, also known as *The Rock Garden.*

Mary Elizabeth Jane Colter (1869–1958) was the Santa Fe Railroad architect commissioned by the Fred Harvey Company to design the now historic Grand Canyon South Rim buildings, which include Hopi House, Hermits Rest, Lookout Studio, Bright Angel Lodge (followed the Bright Angel Hotel), the Indian Watchtower at Desert View, Victor and Colter Halls, and the Inner Canyon's world famous, or "phamous," Phantom Ranch.

Zane Grey accompanied Charles Jesse (Buffalo) Jones to the North Rim to participate in roping mountain lions for zoos. In 1924, Grey authored *Roping Lions in the Grand Canyon.* In the Mogollon Rim area, southeast of Flagstaff, Arizona, twelve of Grey's novels were written in a cabin that he built in 1920.

John Hance, the "great Grand Canyon teller of tall tales," was born in Tennessee. He became the first male Caucasian resident of the canyon, circa 1883, by settling near Grand View Point, 10 aerial miles southeast of today's Grand Canyon Village.

Old-timer. John Hance ca 1918. GRCA 3675

Hance Camp became the end-of-the-line for stagecoach service arriving from Flagstaff, Arizona. After Hance sold his property to the Santa Fe Stage Line, he was compensated by the Fred Harvey Company to tell his stories at El Tovar Hotel. Hance would tell visitors that "he dug the Grand Canyon himself." When asked what he did with all the dirt, he stated, "I piled it near Flagstaff ... what is called the San Francisco Peaks" (elevation 12,670 feet). He also told a woman, "God made the canyon that way to keep trespassers out." In 1919, the year Grand Canyon National Park was established, Hance passed away at Flagstaff, Arizona. He was interred at Grand Canyon Pioneer Cemetery. Rough Rider Buckey O'Neill wrote, *God made the canyon and John Hance the trails. Neither would be complete without the other.*

Jacob Hamblin became known as the "leatherstocking of the west," made famous by James Fennimore Copper's *Leatherstocking Tales*, because of his association with the many Indian tribes of Utah and Arizona. In 1862, Hamblin and party had made a complete circuit around Grand Canyon.

Fred Harvey was an entrepreneur in the true spirit of the word. Harvey was born in London, England, on June 27, 1836. He arrived in New York via a sailing vessel and retained a job as dishwasher that earned him $2.00 per week. There, he recognized early in his endeavors that there was a lack in the food service industry—specifically along travel routes. After saving sufficient funds to travel to New Orleans, he sought work in excellent hotels where he served his own apprenticeship in the hospitality trade. In 1858, Harvey owned his first restaurant in St. Louis, Missouri, and began the service-to-customer tradition that made him the hospitality industry leader. In that respect, he learned that the Santa Fe Railroad would recognize his talent for providing optimum food service and hospitality. The railroad retained Harvey as their key figure in satisfying weary travelers and revamping the meager accommodations in these early days of travel. In 1876, Harvey entered a food service agreement with the Santa Fe Railroad and bought the café inside the Topeka, Kansas, depot. When El Tovar opened in 1905, the Santa Fe retained the newly forming Fred Harvey Company directed by surviving sons Ford, who named the company, and Byron, and son-in-law John Huckel.

Grand Canyoneering: Now a National Historic Landmark, the Kolb Studio was built by the Kolb brothers, Ellsworth and Emery Kolb, starting in 1903. Located at the head of the South Rim's Bright Angel Trail, the first wing of today's five-story studio was constructed on grounds first claimed by era land baron Ralph Cameron.

The studio was enlarged several times up until 1926 with the addition of the auditorium. In 1963, the National Park Service acquired the property for $65,000 with the condition that the surviving brother, Emery, retain use of the studio for home and business until his passing. After that time, the studio befittingly became an outlying addition of the Grand Canyon Association.

Top: **Clutching the South Rim.** Kolb Studio. GRCA D0296
Above: **On the back porch.** The Kolbs, Emery and Blanche, and the Kolb Studio in its early phase, ca 1904. GRCA 4896

William Randolph Hearst's association with Grand Canyon began in 1887 when he stocked cattle ranches near Williams, Arizona. In 1913, 10 aerial miles southeast of Grand Canyon Village, Hearst acquired the Grand View Hotel and Horseshoe Mesa property from Peter D. Berry. Hearst's desire was to develop the area as a major tourist destination in the then-infant Grand Canyon tourist trade. When the Fred Harvey Company secured a concessionaire contract, Hearst declined his land development.

Grand Canyoneering: Originally located between the San Francisco Peaks and the Grand Canyon, the Red Horse Station (photo page 130) was designed as a stagecoach relay point built at Red Horse Wash and Lockwood Canyon in the 1890s. In 1902, the station was moved log-unit-by-log-unit by Grand Canyon pioneer Ralph Cameron and crew and remodeled as the two-story Cameron Hotel. In 1935, architect Mary Colter rescued the station, along with the nearby single-story Buckey O'Neill Cabin, from a scheduled razing and integrated them into the facilities of the Bright Angel Lodge.

Untamed luxury. Cameron Hotel, 1933. GRCA 669

The Kolb Brothers, Ellsworth and Emery, respectively arrived at Grand Canyon in 1901 and 1902. For 75 years, residents and tourists associated the Kolbs with professional photography. Ellsworth and Emery purchased a photography firm in Williams, Arizona, from a Mr. Arbogast for $425 in a year-long monthly installment payment plan. In 1903, the Williams shop was moved to the South Rim, where the Kolbs embarked on a full-time photography business and photographed Bright Angel Trail mule trains and patrons. It was usually Emery who would run down the trail to Indian Garden, where the fresh water of Garden Creek could be used for photo processing. The pictures would be ready for sale on the return of the mule trains. Emery would often beat the mule train down to Indian Garden and would also have to beat the mule train back to the South Rim in eagerness to sell the photographs.

Between 1911 and the beginning of 1912, the Kolb Brothers made a historic and innovative traverse of the Colorado River System with two custom-made boats from the Racine Boat Company of Wisconsin. Even though the science of motion pictures was still unrefined, the two brothers documented their river journey with a Pathé brand movie camera. The first set of Kolb Brother films were printed by Hollywood film producer Cecil B. DeMille, who was famous for motion pictures such as *Gone With the Wind.* Their river journey-adventure was shown and personally narrated by Emery at the Kolb Studio for more than 60 years. Ellsworth passed away in 1960. Emery ran the Colorado River rapids in 1974, at the age of 93, before passing away in 1976.

Top: **Well-groomed.** The Buckey O'Neill Cabin transitions into a Bright Angel Lodge guest room, 1935. GRCA 628
Above: **Photo finish.** The Kolb Studio darkroom, 1976. GRCA 6286

John Doyle Lee established the Lees Ferry Colorado River crossing, located between Grand Canyon Natonal Park's easternmost region and the lowlands of western Glen Canyon. Here it was possible to access the river by horse and wagon, which enabled pioneers to travel by ferry.

William Owen "Buckey" O'Neill arrived in the Arizona Territory in 1879 at the age of 19. O'Neill filed copper claims 20 miles southwest of the Grand Canyon, in the canyon at Indian Garden, and in the vicinity of Yaki Point. His nickname, "Buckey," was earned while playing the card game of faro, in which players bet against the dealer on the cards he will draw from a dealing box. O'Neill would regularly bet all money brought to the table—called, "bucking the tiger." Buckey O'Neill was a member of the Rough Riders unit under the command of then Lieutenant Colonel Theodore Roosevelt.

Grand Canyoneering: Historic to Grand Canyon National Park, ranger cabins, also called snowshoe cabins, were built between 1921 and 1925. The cabins had the key purpose to serve as a base for ranger patrol and anyone in need of shelter—especially on the North Rim where the winters are severe. Cabins built in 1921 include Grand View, Hermit Basin, Pipe Creek, Rowe Well, and Salt Creek. Cabins built in 1925 include Greenland Seep, Kanabownitz Spring, Muav Saddle, and Dry Park.

Top: **Fragile setting.** Muav Saddle Cabin after wildfire, North Rim, 1989. GRCA 16517
Above: **Snowshoe cabin.** Kanabownitz Spring Cabin, North Rim. Notice the angled exterior support beams to handle snow accumulation. ca 1934. GRCA 874

Timothy H. O'Sullivan began his career in the Union's Civil War photography team headed by Matthew Brady. O'Sullivan photographed the Grand Canyon with Lt. George Wheeler, beginning in 1871. This places O'Sullivan several months ahead of the Grand Canyon photography produced by Major John Wesley Powell's crew member, John Hillers.

James T. "Uncle Jim" Owens received his appointment as warden of the Grand Canyon Game Reserve when President Theodore Roosevelt created the reserve in 1906. Originally from Texas, Uncle Jim had the responsibility of protecting the area deer herds from natural predators, particularly mountain lions and wolves. Owens was also the head guide during Roosevelt's 1913 Kaibab Plateau lion hunting trek. Roosevelt's nephew Nicholas said of Owens, *Uncle Jim was a crack shot, with a revolver as well as a rifle ... at home in the forest, wise in the ways of the wilderness, self-reliant, resourceful, tough, almost indestructible.*

Master canyoneer. "Uncle" Jim Owens (second from left), North Rim, 1913. GRCA 5281

Sanford Rowe with partner Ed Hamilton sought to enter the Grand Canyon tourist trade by developing a campground. Led by Havasupai Indian "Big Jim," Rowe was directed to an area where water near the surface created moist ground. Regionally rare Rowe Well, located 2 aerial miles southwest of Grand Canyon Village, was positioned over the site. Because Rowe had an interest in tourism and had already used his homesteading rights in Williams, Arizona, he was able to establish residency and his stagecoach-supported camp by forming the mining claims, Highland Mary, Little Mamie, and the Lucky Strike. The claims were substantiated to officials by Rowe's persuasive accumulation of ore at his smelter. Ultimately, Rowe's camp was bypassed by the railroad as it progressed to the southeast and to the hotels and lodges of the South Rim. In 1956, the Rowe sites were acquired by the National Park Service. Rowe Well Road was named in commemoration of the area. It is located at the beginning of the Hermit Road, west of the Bright Angel Trail.

Pack train. Theodore Roosevelt (in back), North Rim, 1913. GRCA 5281

Grand Canyoneering: Verkamp's Curios opened next door to El Tovar Hotel in 1906. Because water was a rare commodity in these early days at Grand Canyon Village, Verkamp's Curios was designed to capture rain water and snow melt from the roof where it would drain into a cistern, outfitted with a pump, under the porch.

A building that matches a dream. Self-sufficient Verkamp's Curios. Now a Grand Canyon Visitor Center. GRCA D04296VK

Seth Benjamin Tanner was a Mormon settler who established Tanner's Crossing in 1875 at a ford in the Little Colorado River at present-day Cameron, Arizona. The town is located at the junction of Arizona State Highway 64 and U.S. Highway 89, east of Grand Canyon National Park. Tanner built a small house and prospected the immediate and surrounding eastern Grand Canyon area, where he discovered copper deposits. In 1880, he organized the Little Colorado River Mining District. With Franklin French, Tanner improved a Native American route, used by the Ancestral Puebloan and both the

Navajo (Diné) and the Hopi, which became known as the Tanner-French Trail. This is the easternmost established rim-to-river route from the South Rim. The original trailhead was located in the east fork of Tanner Canyon. Today, the trailhead is located at the Desert View–East Rim Drive's Lipan Point approach road.

John George Verkamp arrived at Grand Canyon from Cincinnati, Ohio, in 1898. In the beginning of his career, Verkamp sold curios for the Babbitt Brothers Trading Company from a tent that was located next to the Bright Angel Hotel. Because tourism was not yet thriving, sales were very low. In 1901, after selling his interest to hotel owner Martin Buggeln, Verkamp returned to Ohio. However, in 1905, with passenger train service now four years established and El Tovar Hotel newly constructed, Verkamp returned to the South Rim in the same area and constructed a wood-shingled two-story curio shop with living quarters located above the sales floor. Marking the end of an era in 2008, the National Park Service chose not to renew the shop's sales permit. The shop is now a visitor center.

The Visitor Center was originally built to function as Park Headquarters at the South Rim, as part of the Mission 66 National Parks improvement project. Until the year 2000, the facility administered all park functions, such as dispensing visitor information and backcountry permits and housing the museum collection and research library. Today, the building serves as Park Headquarters and research library while the other functions, which include the Division of Science and Resource Management, have their individual sites. **Canyon View Information Plaza** opened in October of 2000 and is located south of Mather Point. Services include a National Park Service-staffed information desk and auditorium. Ironically, the Grand Canyon cannot be seen from the Canyon View Information Plaza.

Requesting a hiking permit. The Backcountry Office service window in the original Visitor Center courtyard, 1980. GRCA 11001

Travel planner. Canyon View Information Plaza, South Rim Visitor Center, began service in 2000. GRCA

The Yavapai Observation Station, the park's geology museum, is located 1 aerial mile east of the South Rim's El Tovar Hotel at Yavapai Point, at an elevation of 7,200 feet. Formerly called the Yavapai Museum, the structure was funded by the Laura Spelman Rockefeller Foundation and constructed in 1928. The station is equipped with polarized picture windows, like sunglasses, and is oriented to provide supreme Main Corridor viewing. The Yavapai Observation Station is also the location of the National Park Service's 24-hour "web-cam" and is also the location of an annual gathering of amateur astronomers. The Grand Canyon Star Party was founded in 1991 by Dean Ketelsen and is supported by the National Park Service and the Tucson Amateur Astronomers Association.

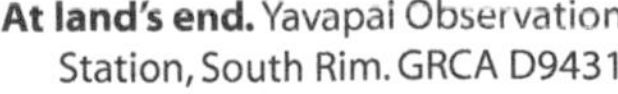

At land's end. Yavapai Observation Station, South Rim. GRCA D9431

Bright Angel Lodge of the South Rim was designed by Mary Colter in 1916 but not built until 1935. The lodge was built at the cost of $500,000, which reflected the pace of inflation, as the neighboring and more magnificent El Tovar Hotel cost half that amount in 1905. As an indication of the momentum of Grand Canyon tourism, the Fred Harvey Company dedicated the building funds during the Great Depression. Colter incorporated the historic Buckey O'Neill Cabin, built in the 1890s, in the design of the lodge. The lobby's history room includes a 10-foot-high fireplace built by Ed Cummings, who used native rock selected by Grand Canyon naturalist Edwin McKee. The fireplace displays the sequential top-to-bottom layers of the Grand Canyon.

Grand Canyoneering: The Stone Shelter at Santa Maria Spring is located 2 trail miles below the South Rim on the Hermit Trail. The natural stone and timber structure was constructed in 1913 at the perennial water source to lend traveler support to Hermit Camp.

The Hermit Trail is one of the least difficult wilderness trails of the named routes. Nevertheless, an apprenticeship should be carried out on the Bright Angel–River Trails and the South and North Kaibab Trails before encountering these non-maintained routes in Grand Canyon.

Above: **Western hospitality.** Bright Angel Lodge, South Rim. GRCA D1458
Right: **Geological fireplace.** Bright Angel Lodge History Room, 1993. GRCA 16104

The Bright Angel Ranger Station was located on the North Rim at an elevation of 8,250 feet, near the North Kaibab Trail. On Grand Canyon maps that show a 1927 date, the ranger station was located in what is now the historic district.

El Tovar Hotel, located at an elevation of 6,866 feet on the South Rim in Grand Canyon Village, was designed by Charles F. Whittlesey of Chicago, Illinois. The

Tucked between the pines. North Rim Entrance Station, 1930. GRCA 3884

In the depth of winter. Bright Angel Ranger Station, North Rim, 1931. GRCA 142

Grand Canyoneering: The Grand Canyon Depot is 2.5 stories tall. The logs used in construction are "squared" on three sides, forming flush support surfaces for the log above and flat interior walls. Custom wrought-iron hardware was made for the depot, and the original doors remain with the letters *GC* cast into the face of the doorknobs. The "Grand Canyon" lettering in the gable is made of copper and originally read "Grand Canon," reflective of Spanish exploration, but was changed in 1911. The lettering was once painted white so as to stand out against the color of the building.

four-story hotel opened on January 14, 1905. Bright Angel Tavern was a candidate name for the new building that would be an immingling of the rustic lodge style adopted by the National Park Service and a Swiss chalet, with its overhanging eaves. Water for the South Rim, even today, is a precious commodity. Spring water for the new hotel came by railroad tank car from Bellemont, Arizona, which is 90 miles south of Grand Canyon between Williams and Flagstaff. The drinking water was filtered and then distilled before going into the hotel.

Top: **100 year anniversary.** El Tovar Hotel (1905-2005). GRCA D0514
Above: **Extraordinary accommodations.** El Tovar Hotel at age three, 1908. GRCA 15523

The hotel, built by the Santa Fe Railroad, was named in commemoration of the Spanish explorer Don Pedro de Tovar. Originally, the company specified a 50-room structure, but ultimately authorized a 100-room structure, budgeted at what would today seem a low price of $250,000. The expansion to 100 rooms would create hospitality accommodations for 250 guests. Timber used in the construction was imported from the state of Oregon and the foundation, entryway, and chimney were made of native Kaibab Limestone Formation rock. The hotel's great rooms include the Rotunda, the Rendezvous, and the Music Solarium.

The expense of the hotel did not include the $20,000 state-of-the-art sewage system. Environmental care was taken in 1905 to install an antiseptic system, in which the waste traveled through underground pipes to concrete tanks where the solid material decomposed. The remaining fluids passed through eight filter fields and then flowed into the ground appearing as water with no odor.

The Farlee Hotel, also known as the Diamond Creek Hotel, was located at Diamond Creek near the town of Peach Springs, Arizona. This was the first Grand

Canyon hotel, which was built and operated by Julius and Cecilia Farlee from 1883–1889, not only at Grand Canyon, but in the canyon itself. Access to the clean but roughhewn, eight bedroom, two-story hotel was by a stagecoach from the railroad at Peach Springs.

The Grand Canyon Railroad Depot, located on a 20-acre site south of the South Rim's El Tovar Hotel, was designed by Francis Wilson of Santa Barbara, California. Built between 1909 and 1910 by the Atchison, Topeka and Santa Fe Railroad under the Grand Canyon Railway subsidiary, the main floor served as passenger and freight facilities, including a ticket office, waiting room, baggage room, and additional utility rooms. The staircase led to the railway agent living quarters, where there are two bedrooms, kitchen and pantry, living room, and lavatory. Akin to El Tovar Hotel, the log-constructed depot fit the western theme that the Santa Fe was presenting to the passenger arriving at Grand Canyon. Days gone by, this rustic depot was the traveler's first impression of the Grand Canyon setting. There were approximately fourteen log depots constructed in the United States. Grand Canyon Depot is one of the three structures that remain.

Ambience by Santa Fe. Grand Canyon Depot, 1939. GRCA 667

Grand Canyon Inn, as it was ultimately named by the final owner, a Ms. Jacobs, was located 1 aerial mile west of the South Rim's El Tovar Hotel at Maricopa Point, elevation 6,900 feet. The inn, which was originally named the Grand Canyon Trading Post, was built in 1936 by Grand Canyon pioneer Daniel Hogan on the property of his Lost Orphan Mine. This was a very good location, as the Santa Fe Railroad had the Hermit Rim Road and Hermits Rest established and in full operation. Hogan was able to capture a market share as tourists traveled between the El Tovar Hotel and the end of the 8-mile drive to Hermits Rest. At one time it was also called the Kachina Lodge. After Will Rogers Jr. acquired the property in 1949, the inn was renamed Rogers' Place.

Grand Canyon Lodge was built between 1927 and 1928, on the very brink of the North Rim at Bright Angel Point, by the Utah Parks Company—a subsidiary of the Union Pacific Railroad. The architect was Gilbert Stanley Underwood, who also designed the Ahwahnee hotel in Yosemite National Park, California. The

Songs of farewell. Employees "singing away" tour busses at Grand Canyon Lodge, North Rim, 1930. GRCA 504

Snowed in. Grand Canyon Lodge, ca 1941. GRCA 1275

Backdraft. Grand Canyon Lodge after disastrous 4 A.M. kitchen fire, 1932. GRCA 579

Utah Parks Company used the lodge as a terminal point in the bus tours that brought visitors to Grand Canyon, Bryce, and Zion National Parks. Literally, a tour could travel no farther south. The end of the line is the circular drive in front of the lodge, immediately on the other side of which are the depths of the canyon. The lodge burned down as a result of a disastrous kitchen fire in 1932 and was rebuilt in 1936. Picture windows in the dining and the Sun Room offer dramatically vast canyon views. To the east of the main lobby is an auditorium. Directly under the Sun Room is the open-air space locally termed Moon Room. Attached to the parent structure are a curio shop, bookstore, and post office.

The Grand View Hotel was built in 1892 by Peter D. Berry. Based on his copper mining claim, the hotel was located 10 aerial miles southeast of today's Grand Canyon Village. When the Bright Angel Hotel (predecessor to Bright Angel Lodge) was constructed, it became Grand View's principal competitor. After the railroad reached the South Rim in 1901, the Grand View Hotel experienced

Bits of broken window glass remain. Grand View Hotel, South Rim, 1899. GRCA 990

severe profit loss as this new area of Grand Canyon Village began to develop. The hotel went out of business in 1916 and was razed in 1929. Today, structure remnants include window and bottle fragments and bits of hardware. Even though the hotel has long been gone, the logs that were used in its construction can still be seen. They were salvaged and donated by Grand View property owner William Randolph Hearst to the Indian Watchtower project at Desert View. The hotel logs make up the ceiling of the "kiva" room.

Grand Canyoneering: Hull Cabin is located 10 aerial miles southeast of the South Rim's El Tovar Hotel. The cabin was built in 1888 as home and ranch for brothers Phillip and William Hull, who herded cattle and kept sheep. The site also includes a barn and the nearby reliable water source Hull Tank. The Hulls were the earliest settlers and recognized the tourist trade early on. The brothers partnered with famed Grand Canyon storyteller, John Hance, in a stagecoach operation that provided traveler service from Flagstaff, Arizona.

Photo by Flood Hefley

Territorial ranch. Hull Cabin, Kaibab National Forest, South Rim.

Timbered entrance. Hermits Rest, South Rim. GRCA T06

Hermits Rest is located on the rim 4 aerial miles west of the South Rim's El Tovar Hotel at an elevation of 6,650 feet. The National Historic Landmark was designed by architect Mary Colter and built in 1914. In one technique to make the building appear old when first built, the fireplace was deliberately blemished with soot. Colter acquired the entrance bell from a mission in New Mexico and the lantern by the fireplace was originally hanging outside to symbolize "welcome." The rustic interior and the built-in-to-the-earth exterior were created through the intentional use of trained builders who used boulders and timbers in a fashion that appears untrained.

Low doors and rough-hewn ladders. Hopi House, South Rim. GRCA D03551

Hopi House was built in 1905 and is a National Historic Landmark located east of El Tovar Hotel in the South Rim's Grand Canyon Village. Designed by architect Mary Colter, Hopi House is a pueblo-reminiscent building reflective of the life and art of the Native Americans, based on the ancient Hopi city of Oraibi. Hopi Indians were invited to live at Hopi House to work at their arts for mutual benefit and visitor appreciation. Native American dance at the outdoor platform tapered off between 1959 and 1972. One of the Hopi terms for Grand Canyon is *Tokpela*, meaning "endless space."

The Indian Watchtower at Desert View (Desert View Watchtower, also Watchtower at Desert View) is located 18 aerial miles east of the South Rim's El Tovar Hotel, adjacent to the East Entrance Station and the Desert View–East Rim Drive. The Indian Watchtower was designed by architect Mary Colter and built in 1932 as a tourist destination. There are various names for the structure. Written

Above: **Desert views—about 100 miles worth.** The Indian Watchtower at Desert View provides 360-degree panoramas behind and into the Grand Canyon's vast interior and far past into the Painted Desert and the Navajo Indian Reservation. GRCA D4325
Right: **Inside-up.** The Indian Watchtower. GRCA TDVi02

by Mary Colter in 1933, the *Manual for Drivers and Guides Descriptive of the Indian Watchtower at Desert View and Its Relation, Architecturally, to the Prehistoric Ruins of the Southwest* best describes Mary Colter's intended site name as the tower was patterned after those at Hovenweep National Monument and at Mesa Verde National Park. The Santa Fe Railroad bridge department produced the steel framework, which is concealed by unquarried native rock. The idea was to compliment the structure with the surroundings using rock from the native Kaibab Limestone Formation. The light-colored exterior and protruding wall stone, *Balolookong*, represents the Hopi Indian's mythical Great White Serpent. The ground floor represents a kiva, and the logs in the ceiling were donated by William

Randolph Hearst from his razed Grand View Hotel. The staircase ascends to the Hopi Room, which was painted by Fred Kabotie and was themed after the Hopi Snake Dance—or "Rain Dance." The two upper galleries were "rock art" painted by Fred Harvey Company artist Fred Geary. The elevation of the land at the site is 7,438 feet. The 30-foot wide by 70-foot tall tower increased the mean elevation to 7,508 feet, making it the highest prominence on the South Rim. The neighboring Navajo Point features the highest natural land elevation of 7,498 feet.

Grand Canyoneering: Fire Lookout Towers are centrally located and rise above the trees to observe the transition zone between the Kaibab National Forest and the Grand Canyon National Park. The tallest regional, steel-frame, Aermoter Company tower is on the North Rim in the Kaibab National Forest. The cab of the Dry Park tower is 120 feet above the forest floor.

The Osborne Fire Finder system, a circular regional map each site is outfitted with, is used by United States Forest Service Fire Lookouts, such as Mark Guyman at Jacob Lake, Arizona, to determine exact fire locations. An occupational hazard inherent with the job is lightning strikes. While observing the forest in August of 2002, Mark's copper wire-grounded tower was struck while he was sitting on an insulated chair. (A wooden stool with telephone pole glass insulators screwed into the feet.) Mark said:

I noticed that there was a quiet unlike any other quiet. Later I realized my radio worked perfectly. No static and all voices were clear... the lightning had fixed all the connections.

Photo by Flood Hefley

Photo by Flood Hefley

Top: **Sky scraper.** Jacob Lake Fire Tower, North Rim.
Above: **Deep sky.** Above the old-growth Kaibab National Forest from the cabin of Jacob Lake Fire Tower, North Rim.

The Kaibab Lodge, elevation 8,770 feet, is located adjacent to Arizona State Highway 67, outside Grand Canyon National Park, 15 aerial miles northwest of the North Rim's Grand Canyon Lodge. The Kaibab Lodge was built circa 1926 and is a former cattle ranch and tourist camp, which was operated by Will S. Rust—the brother of North Rim Grand Canyon tourist pioneer, David Dexter Rust. Today, from mid May to the beginning of November, the lodge is available as a rustic tourist destination.

Fred Kabotie. Interior artist of The Indian Watchtower and creator of the Hopi Room's Snake Alter sand painting, ca 1932. GRCA 8307

On the threshold. The Lookout Studio, South Rim. GRCA D1457

The Lookout Studio was built in 1914 and designed by architect Mary Colter and is a National Historic Landmark. The studio–gift shop is located immediately west of the Bright Angel Lodge and is made of native stone to blend in with the South Rim. The studio was originally built not only to compete for business with the Kolb Brothers and their studio, but was intentionally located in its place to confuse the unsuspecting visitor. The typical visitor thought they were at the Kolb Studio and went no farther to the west where the Kolb Brothers had their studio at the head of the Bright Angel Trail.

Moqui Lodge and Camp were located 8 aerial miles south of the South Rim's El Tovar Hotel, outside Grand Canyon National Park on an 80-acre site in the Kaibab National Forest. Preceding Moqui Lodge, Rudolph Kirby constructed a campground and store in 1928. In 1930, the site was bought by George Kimes who augmented it with cabins. After the property changed hands two more times, the camp was purchased in 1976 by the Grand Canyon National Park concessionaire Amfac. This holding then transferred to Xanterra. At this time the lodgings included an A-frame main building and hotel-style rooms. Ultimately, the site was cleared due to out-of-code structures. The land was re-seeded with a United States Forest Service indigenous seed mix, and to the untrained eye it is as if the lodge never existed.

Grand Canyoneering: Some of Phantom Ranch's eventful years were in the 1960s, when continual ranger service began and a generator replaced lanterns. In 1966, electricity arrived, which enabled summer cooling and winter heating. In 1970, purified drinking water came with the completion of the Trans-Canyon Water Line. (Today, Phantom Ranch consumes 7,000 gallons of water per summer day). *The Phamous Phantom Ranch Stew* recipe is concocted and served to dudes and hikers. In 1976, four dormitories were built in a style that matches architect Mary Colter's original design. In 1981, the revegetation program was put in effect in response to increased visitation.

O'Neill Cabin, located immediately west of the Bright Angel Lodge and named for William Owen "Buckey" O'Neill, was built in the 1890s and stands as one of the oldest structures in Grand Canyon National Park.

Phantom Ranch is located 7 aerial miles southwest of the North Rim's Grand Canyon Lodge and .25 mile north of the Colorado River on a 14-acre parcel along Bright Angel Creek. In the past, the holding was designated **Rust's Camp** after pioneer and entrepreneur David Rust. Rust's Camp found its beginnings in the early 1900s when promoters in Utah viewed the North Rim as a potential tourist destination. Using horses, Edwin Dilworth Wooley, "Uncle Dee," established the Grand Canyon Transportation Company in 1903 and employed his son-in-law David Rust as proprietor. The ranch was renamed **Roosevelt Camp** after Theodore Roosevelt came through in 1913 on his way to engage

The Canteen. Where dudes, river runners, and hikers draw together at Phantom Ranch, Bright Angel Canyon. GRCA

Ranger Station: What historic buildings can I find in the North Rim area, other than the Grand Canyon Lodge? In the rim vicinity, you'll find the Grand Canyon Lodge District. The lodge was originally built between 1927 and 1928 and rebuilt in 1936 after a ravaging kitchen fire in 1932. Also found in the area are railroad resort-period support buildings and the nine "Log Cabins" that were built in 1929 and remodeled in 1947.

The Headquarters District includes the Trail Crew Bunkhouse, built in 1935; the Fire Management Office, built in 1925 (moved to its present location in 1935); the Ranger Offices, built in 1924; and the Firehouse-Ambulance Facility, built in 1934.

In the Campground District, you'll find one of the earliest auto service stations in the state of Arizona—the Gas and Oil Station, built in 1933. This service station should not be confused with the (almost historic) gas station built in 1947.

Cabin restored. One of the oldest in the region, the two-room Jacob Lake Ranger Station was built in 1910 for a base of horseback ranger patrol in the Kaibab Forest, North Rim.

in a mountain lion hunt on the North Rim. The "dude ranch" was designed and named by architect Mary Colter, who in 1922 enjoyed the opening celebration with her sister Harriet. The original cabins and dining hall, called the Canteen, were built from both local materials and materials imported by mule. The ranch can accommodate 92 guests. A hint of snow is possible every year at the streamside desert setting of Phantom Ranch and the extended Inner Canyon. In the exceptional year of 1939, the ranch received 11 inches of snow.

Photos by Flood Hefley

Incognito. Red Horse Station inconspicuously huddled within the cabins of the Bright Angel Lodge. In the days of stagecoaching to Grand Canyon (see text pages 99 and 112), the Red Horse Station was amended by the Moqui Station, which provided for a reliable location to water horses en route to the South Rim from Flagstaff, Arizona.

Archaeologists, Historians, Scientists, Naturalists, and Artists

Grand Canyoneering: Ferdinand "Ferde" Grofe composed the 1930 *Grand Canyon Suite*. The five movements are "Sunrise," "The Painted Desert," "On the Trail," "Sunset," and "Cloudburst." In 1917, Grofe made his first Grand Canyon visit. Thereafter, he was at Grand Canyon frequently until 1926. In explaining how he formulated the piece, Grofe said:

I saw color, but I heard it, too.

Dr. Robert Clark Euler was appointed Grand Canyon National Park research anthropologist by Senator Barry Goldwater in 1974. Dr. Euler is probably best known for his work with split-twig figurine animal effigies and the excavation of Stanton's Cave in Marble Canyon. The Arizona Power Commission contracted Dr. Euler to conduct a survey of archaeological sites in Marble Canyon along the Colorado River by helicopter prior to their assignment of an official dam site—now Glen Canyon Dam in Glen Canyon. During these 1960s surveys in Marble Canyon, Euler documented more than 200 archaeological sites. Dr. Euler is also known for drafting the Memorandum of Understanding for the use of Havasupai Traditional Use Lands. This was used as part of the Grand Canyon National Park Enlargement Act of 1975 as established by President Gerald Ford. Dr. Euler said, *There are many important circumstances about the archaeology of Grand Canyon. One is that during the Archaic Period, 3,000 to 4,000 years ago, there were Indians roaming around and placing effigies in caves. The effigies are animal figurines that are made of split-twigs. These people were hoping for a good hunt. We found hundreds of these hidden away in the caves that are difficult to get to in the canyon. That's the main thing we know about the Archaic Period. We really don't know who these people were or where they came from or why they left—they are somewhat isolated in time.*

Yet to be decoded. Split-twig figurine made from a single willow or cottonwood tree shoot. GRCA 4684

Bruce Aiken was the resident pump master at Roaring Springs from 1973 to 2006. His duties included maintaining the system that supplies water up to the North Rim's 4 million gallon holding tanks, and then into the Trans-Canyon Water Line and across the Colorado River to Indian Garden, where it is then pumped up to the South Rim's 14 million gallon holding tanks. While Bruce Aiken lived in the canyon with his wife and children, he studied the intricacies of Grand Canyon. He is a foremost landscape painter of this favorite subject.

Louis Benton Akin is among the first noted Grand Canyon artists to be exhibited nationally. Of his 125 works, some 30 paintings are of the Grand Canyon. Akin was living among the Hopi when he was awarded a commission by the Santa Fe Railroad in 1903 to paint landscapes that included the Hopi. Well liked by the tribe, he was inducted into their secret society and given the name *Mapli*, meaning "sleeveless," for the style of shirt that he wore.

Evening Grand Canyon, one of his notable works, was painted on a colossal 9-foot by 6-foot canvas and is displayed on the inside east wall of the South Rim's Verkamp's Curios gift shop (now a National Park Service visitor center). The painting was declined for show at New York's National Academy of Art due to its size. After Akin failed to sell the painting, he was determined to cut it up and reuse the canvas. He had strayed from the Native American genre, his true expertise, and was trying unsuccessfully to establish himself as a landscape painter. Funds were tight. Akin must have been conflicted, however, because he never got around to cutting up the canvas. After Akin's passing in 1913, John Verkamp bought the painting for the curio shop.

Grand Canyoneering: Edwin Dinwiddie McKee began as a seasonal naturalist under Grand Canyon National Park naturalist Glen Sturdevant. McKee assumed the permanent position in 1929 when Sturdevant drowned in the Colorado River's Horn Creek Rapid, located directly below the South Rim's Grand Canyon Village. Serving until 1940, Mckee expanded the ranger Interpretive Program to include campfire sessions and guided geology walks to the bottom of the canyon. In 1964, he tutored Apollo 11 and other Apollo program astronauts, including Neil Armstrong and Jim Lovell, to prepare for the identification of lunar geology.

Ranger naturalist. Edwin McKee with a pigmy nuthatch bird in his hand. Notice the bird's shadow on McKee's shirt. GRCA 1436

John Burroughs visited the Grand Canyon in 1909 with fellow naturalist John Muir and rode by mule a snow-covered Bright Angel Trail. In reaction to the grandeur, Burroughs called the canyon *The Divine Abyss.*

Marguerite Henry authored the 1953 book, *Brighty of the Grand Canyon,* and with it won the William Allen White award for the story and quality of writing. The tale was conceived when Henry was delivered a magazine article dated 1923 from a librarian named Miss Lathrop. The account revealed a real burro that lived in the canyon and interacted with such people as North Rim Game Warden, "Uncle" Jim Owens, and President Theodore Roosevelt. A Peter Jepson bronze statue of

Brighty is in the North Rim's Grand Canyon Lodge Sun Room. Out of the more than 30 books created by Marguerite Henry, she wrote to this author, "Brighty is one of my favorites."

George Wharton James authored more than 50 books on the American West, including *In and Around the Grand Canyon*, written in 1900. James writes, *This book is a growth of ten years' visits. Hence it is not an ordinary book ... but the accumulated result of renewed visits and many explorations. This book was written in the darkness of the night in the depths of the Canyon ... on the driver's seat or inside the jolting stage ... in the heart of a fierce storm on the Painted Desert ... wearied out, waiting for water and a horse, stretched on the sand, with the fierce roar of the Colorado River in my ear ... under the trees at Lee's Ferry ... baking in the sun ... anywhere, everywhere ... a part of this book was born.*

Dr. Clinton Hart Merriam, most often referred to as C. Hart Merriam, was a Department of Agriculture scientist who recognized the Grand Canyon as a self-contained institution of the Earth's history. In this relatively small area, Merriam identified 6 of the 7 classic life zones, which include the Sonoran, at river level, the Upper Sonoran, the Transition, the Canadian, the Hudsonian, the Arctic-Alpine, respectively at the San Francisco Peaks summits and the canyon rims. The absent zone is Tropical. To receive the same life zone change experience elsewhere, one would have to travel from Canada to Mexico.

Ranger Station:

"The purpose of netting bats at Phantom Ranch is to look at the area's overall species diversity and abundance with an emphasis put on looking for the western red bat, which is fast losing habitat throughout the Southwest. Also used is an Anabat detector, which records the echolocation calls of bats for positive identification." —Pam Cox, Grand Canyon National Park

Left: **Safety net.** Using expertise, a mist net, and quick reaction time, Grand Canyon National Park's Pam Cox safely handles a pallid bat at Phantom Ranch. Notice the fine-mesh net pattern against Pam's gloves. GRCA

Left below: **Close friend.** Pam Cox with a pallid bat, Phantom Ranch. What is unique to the pallid bat is that it catches its food, primarily insects, almost exclusively on the ground as opposed to while in flight. Because the pallid has such large ears, they are able to detect the sound of their prey's footsteps—like that of a scorpion (the bat is immune to the sting). GRCA

Aerial Trolleys and Man-made Bridges

> **Grand Canyoneering:** Inner Canyon bridges over the Colorado River replaced the David Dexter Rust Cableway, also known as Rust's Cable. "Dead-men," high anchor points of steel or concrete on either side of a bridge, are used to give the span "lift." Bridge deck over-the-water heights vary depending on Glen Canyon water release schedules.

An aerial trolley was located in the canyon 4 aerial miles northeast of the South Rim's El Tovar Hotel. Transportation and utility service began in 1907, the first mechanized travel over the Colorado River using an open-air iron gondola. This was **David Dexter Rust's** windlass cable system, which joined the Old Bright Angel Trail from the North Rim through Bright Angel Canyon with what would become known as the Cable Trail from the southwest. The gondola was suspended 60 feet above the river on a 450-foot long cable and was drawn to-and-from the

Aerial trolley. David Rust's Colorado River crossing. Site now occupied by the Kaibab Suspension Bridge, 1909. GRCA 1462

river banks by a cable that was coiled around metal drums that were used as wheels. On this system in 1913, **Theodore Roosevelt** made a traverse over the Colorado River en route to a hunting expedition on the North Rim. The swinging Bright Angel Suspension Bridge, interchangeably called the Kaibab Bridge, ultimately replaced the aerial trolley in 1921.

The Bass Cableways over the Colorado River were established by Grand Canyon pioneer William Wallace Bass in 1906 to link the North and South Bass Trails, located 20 river miles downstream from David Rust's system. The 1906 installment was a dual-cable without formal cartage over the river. In 1908, Bass added a wood-frame cage to an upgraded four-strand cable system, which had the ability to transport several tourists and a

Top: **Down loading.** Indian Garden Tramway, ca 1931. GRCA 73
Bottom: **Asbestos claim.** William Bass' Hakatai mining camp, 1968. GRCA 5295A

horse or mule. Bill Vaughan operated the system from 1908 to 1920. The first cable was located at river mile 108, at Bass Rapid, and a second system located at river mile 111 at the mouth of Hakatai Canyon, 15 aerial miles northwest of the South Rim's El Tovar Hotel. The original function of the cable crossing was to provide transportation of Bass' asbestos and copper ore. Eventually, the transportation of tourists over the river replaced the ore when Bass shifted his business efforts to tourism.

The Trans-Canyon Tramway was initiated by the San Francisco, California, based engineer George Davol in 1916 and backed by the Santa Fe Railroad and supported by Washington, D.C. Specifications called for a terminal at the South Rim's Hopi Point, west of Grand Canyon Village, and a terminal at Tiyo Point, west of the North Rim's Grand Canyon Lodge. Had the tram been completed, the site would have used the Isis Temple and Dana Butte to support the 7.5-mile long cable system.

Construction was well under way, including the laboriously built, but only partially installed cable. To cross the Colorado River at Horn Creek, a system was established with the aid of an improvised raft of empty ten-gallon oil drums. Trans-Canyon Tramway survey crews slung two burros, "Jack" and "Jill," up and down the sheer cliffs to be used to haul supplies on the intermediate plateaus.

The project was ultimately abandoned due to an intense November snowstorm. The storm set in while the surveyors were already challenged by the precipitous cliffs. After everything, the tramway was vetoed by the Director of the National Park Service, Stephen Mather.

Grand Canyoneering: From the South Rim's Yavapai Observation Station, the Kaibab Suspension Bridge can be seen as a black stripe over the Colorado River.

The Bright Angel Suspension Bridge, sometimes called the Old Bridge or the Old Kaibab Bridge, was built in 1921 over the Colorado River to connect the Old Bright Angel Trail to the Cable Trail (originally the Wash Henry Trail). The swinging bridge was supported by 80-pound railroad track sections, called deadmen, cemented into the canyon walls. The 1,200-pound cables were delivered by eight mules guided by wranglers at each head. The plank-constructed walkway, with a span of 440 feet, was suspended 60 feet above the river. The Bright Angel Suspension Bridge was replaced by the Kaibab Suspension Bridge in 1928.

The Kaibab Suspension Bridge was built in the night under floodlights to escape the heat of the Inner Canyon day and is referred to as the Black Bridge because of its color. Built at the cost of $48,000 in 1928, the ridged bridge is suspended 78 feet above the Colorado River and completes the Kaibab Trail System

Top: **Swinging bridge.** Bright Angel Suspension Bridge, ca 1927. Site now occupied by the Kaibab Suspension Bridge. GRCA 13101
Bottom: **Completing the trail.** Kaibab Suspension Bridge and Suspension Bridge Tunnel—the last installation of the Kaibab Trail System. GRCA D1247

between the North Rim and the South Rim. The bridge is located near Bright Angel Creek and Phantom Ranch and can handle a simultaneous mule train crossing. The dimensions of the bridge dictate that it remain open, as the neighboring Silver Suspension Bridge does not have the width or sidewall height to allow mule passage. In construction, both of the 2,030-pound guying cables were unreeled on the South Rim. To transport the cable down to the site, a mule at each end of the cable had a 200 pound coiled portion fastened to its barrel. Then a team, comprised mostly of Havasupai Indians, shouldered the cable at equal intervals and carried it down the South Kaibab Trail. Concrete plugs, called "dead-men," were formed into the canyon's Inner Gorge to support the eight 1.5-inch diameter steel cables that lift the bridge's 440-foot span. The walkway is a steel and plank combination, which had for time, equine-style rubber floor matting covering the wood to prolong the life of the walkway against the grinding of mule shoes.

Risky endeavor. Men perched on cables constructing the Kaibab Suspension Bridge, 1928. GRCA 10117

Special delivery. Cable "shouldered" down the South Kaibab Trail arrives for Kaibab Suspension Bridge construction, 1928. GRCA 10111

Grand Canyoneering: At the side-by-side location of the Navajo Bridges that were built in 1929 and 1995, twin bridges are revealed. Revealed, also, is almost double vision, as the bridges look almost identical with the exception of a wider deck on the newer bridge. Jerry Cannon, designer of the bridge built in 1995, said of the bridge built in 1929:

We respect the historic Navajo Bridge because its design and construction triumphed over difficult site and technical problems. The major challenges for the second bridge were environmental concerns and coordination with government agencies that didn't even exist when the first bridge was built.

The Silver Suspension Bridge was built in 1965. The rigid bridge carries the Trans-Canyon Water Line over the Colorado River and doubles as a hiker-only footbridge. From the end of the Bright Angel Trail, this "shortcut" alleviates the need to complete travel on the River Trail to the South Kaibab Trail and the Kaibab Suspension Bridge. The Silver Suspension Bridge creates a direct route to the North Kaibab Trail in the close proximity of the Bright Angel Campground. Two conventional steel uprights, called "dead-men," are concrete formed at the bases into the surrounding rock to support the bridge's 522-foot span. The 4-foot 2-inch wide steel grid walkway is see-through and is suspended 35 feet above the river. The construction materials were delivered by helicopter. During the construction period, contractor Elling Halvorson provided sightseeing opportunities via his helicopters, which inspired him to form Papillon Grand Canyon Helicopters. Now based out of Grand Canyon National Park Airport, the helipads were formally located inside the town of Tusayan.

Anchorage. Engineer John Lawrence installing Kaibab Suspension Bridge cable, 1928. GRCA 10121

The Navajo Bridge of 1929 was designed by the Arizona State Highway Commission and built by the Kansas City Structural Steel Company of Missouri. The alternate bridge names are the Marble Canyon Bridge, as it spans Marble Canyon at the easternmost boundary of Grand Canyon National Park; the Lees Ferry Bridge, as it is 4.5 river miles downstream from Lees Ferry, which it replaced; and the general name of The Grand Canyon Bridge (its official name from 1929–1934) because of its proximity to Grand Canyon

National Park. Because the southern approach is on Navajo tribal lands, the bridge was renamed Navajo Bridge in 1934.

Excavation and blasting to prepare the anchoring system began on June 23, 1927, and steel work began in August. Heavy equipment and materials were shipped across the Colorado River by the ferry system. The volume of freight traffic greatly stressed the ferryboat and the cables it used to cross the river. Numerous accidents and deaths came as a result. Three men drowned in high water on June 7, 1928. In the surging river, a Model T Ford with the men on board rolled over and was pinned under the capsized ferryboat. The ferry system was closed shortly thereafter, largely as a result of the tragedy. For the remaining seven months of bridge construction, materials had to be driven hundreds of miles around the canyon network.

The two halves of the cantilevered arch that form the underside of the bridge were joined on September 12, 1928. The two-lane bridge is 834 feet long and 497 feet above the Colorado River. At the cost of $390,000, the bridge required 500 cubic yards of concrete and 2.5 million pounds of steel. The bridge provided service to motorists beginning on January 12, 1929. The historic bridge, now designated for foot traffic only, is 150 feet upstream from the Navajo Bridge of 1995.

The Navajo Bridge of 1995 was designed by Cannon and Associates of Tucson, Arizona, and built by Edward Kraemer and Sons, Inc., of Wisconsin. The purpose of the bridge was to remedy the greater amounts of weight and traffic that were traveling the region and flowing over the historic neighboring bridge. The bridge is 150 feet downstream from the Navajo Bridge of 1929. Preparing the rims for anchoring sites began on October 14, 1994. The four-lane bridge required 1,790 cubic yards of concrete and 3.9 million pounds of steel and went into public service on September 14, 1995. As supervised by Jerry Cannon, the National Park Service required that the Colorado River remain open to boaters who would float under the construction site. To protect endangered plant species (primarily the Copper Canyon milkvetch) the National Park Service also required the project to comply with the Federal Endangered Species Act. The rim anchoring sites could not merely be blasted out, but a rock slice-and-removal technique had to be invented and employed. Under such an operation, catch-nets were hung under the North and South Rims to inhibit natural debris from entering the Colorado River. Taken very seriously from an environmental standpoint, any material that would have entered the river unnaturally, would be considered man tampering with and advancing the erosion process of the Grand Canyon.

The Anasazi Bridge is a series of tree limb poles located 200 feet above the Colorado River that were laid out in catwalk fashion to negotiate a difficult section in the Redwall Limestone Formation. The age-old bridge was discovered by surveyor Gordon Denipah during the exploration of dam sites in Marble Canyon. The Anasazi Bridge is one of two historic bridges in the Grand Canyon. The other was the planking that extended out to **Boysag Point.** *Boysag* is Paiute for "bridge."

Ranger Station:
What was used to cross the Colorado River to Phantom Ranch in the old days? Before the bridge of 1921 and David Rust's aerial trolley, pioneers typically used a rowboat to ferry across the river. A task in itself, it was also an undertaking to swim your mount across from river bank to river bank. Mule, horse, or burro, the mount was tethered to the boat so as not to get swept away and lost in the river's muscular current.

Ledge-to-ledge. The Anasazi Bridge, Marble Canyon. The exact location of the bridge is not given here to preserve site integrity and because "this sensitive site is closed to visitation due to the fragility of the structure and individual loose beams." Ian Hough, Grand Canyon National Park. GRCA

Caves, Caverns, Windows, Natural Bridges, and Arches

Caves, including abandoned mines, require a National Park Service access permit due to the hazards associated with cave features. Hazards include the possibilities of poor visibility, unbreathable or poisonous air, irregular flooring, and potential free falls due to the presence of mine shafts.

Bass Grotto is located on the rim of Bass Canyon at the South Bass Trail 15 aerial miles northwest of the South Rim's El Tovar Hotel. The chamber is in Kaibab Limestone Formation rock. Grand Canyon pioneer William Wallace Bass used the grotto for a variety of purposes including pantry and photography darkroom.

Bat Cave is the location of a bat dung deposit that was excavated for use as a fertilizer called guano. The mining effort included a 2-mile-long tram system that originated on the South Rim and passed over the Colorado River at river mile 266 near Quartermaster Canyon. Starting in the 1940s, the accumulation was hauled by ore car from the north bank of the river to the South Rim at an elevation of 4,803 feet. The ore car was replaced by flatboat and the material was unwieldily hauled 22 river miles downstream to Lake Mead, where it was transferred and sent out for distribution. The tram cable was removed in 1960 after it was hit by an airplane.

Grand Canyoneering: From the North Rim's Bright Angel Point, adjacent to the Grand Canyon Lodge, the flow of Roaring Springs can be heard from 3,000 feet below. Roaring Springs Cave is located in the promontory of Uncle Jim Point. In 1934, Ed Seigel of the Utah Parks Company and National Park Service ranger Albert Turner explored the cave with the aid of gasoline-fueled lanterns. At one point the explorers found a side cavern, stalactites and stalagmites, clusters of calcite crystals, and shallow pools of water. Today, Roaring Springs supplies water to the National Park's thirsty Inner Canyon travelers and the North Rim's four million and the South Rim's fourteen million gallon holding tanks.

The Grand View Caves are located in the Last Chance Mine–Horseshoe Mesa area, 10 aerial miles southeast of the South Rim's El Tovar Hotel. Dome Cave includes stalactites and stalagmites along 1,000 feet of passageway. The feature was discovered in 1896 by Canyon Copper Company cook Joseph Gildner. Alternate names include Cave of the Domes and Crystal Cave.

Rampart Cave was discovered by Willis Evans and is located 37 aerial miles west of the South Rim's El Tovar Hotel at the river level elevation of 2,000 feet. The exact site is

Ice Age confirmation. Rampart Cave, western Grand Canyon, 1938. GRCA 8516

not disclosed to preserve site integrity. In 1937, the Carnegie Institution selected Jerome Douglas "Jerry" Laudermilk to conduct the research of the cave. Laudermilk identified many of the same plants found in the area today, such as maidenhair fern. The cave's contents include the skeletal remains of the giant ground sloth and sloth dung, which disclosed the diet of the sloth and era plants.

Snow-melt energized. Roaring Springs, lower North Rim.
Photo by Flood Hefley

Redwall Cavern is located at river mile 33 in Marble Canyon in Redwall Limestone Formation rock. Where the Colorado River makes a greater than 90 degree bend and crosscuts the south river bank cliff, river level excavation of the large chamber, approximately 300 feet wide by 150 feet deep has taken place. The height depends on where the measurement is taken. As the entrance of the cavern tapers up from the river's edge, the ceiling height of 70 feet decreases from the opening to the rear of the cave.

Refuge Cave is located on the South Rim of Marble Canyon (exact location not disclosed to preserve site integrity) where legend says that Indians defeated by the Navajo traveled down the 2000-foot-deep tunnel and escaped not across, but under the river. Torches, pots, and projectile points were found in the cave. Now mapped, the cave reveals no exit.

Stanton's Cave is located in Marble Canyon 120 feet above the Colorado River, 31 miles downstream from Lees Ferry. In 1889, the cave was used by Robert Brewster Stanton, who surveyed the Colorado River channel as a possible railroad route. The 120-foot-deep cave was used to store survey equipment for a secondary survey effort after the failed first attempt. In 1934, river runners discovered that the cave contained Native American artifacts. The National Park Service recognized the contents as significant, but did not authorize an excavation until 1969. Archaeologist Dr. Robert Euler led the excavation team, which was funded by the National Geographic Society. The cave's artifacts included willow shoot "split-twig" figurines that resemble deer and other animals. The figures confirmed the presence of Archaic Period people. Dr. Euler also found ancient driftwood, several extinct birds, and the remnants of the Herrington mountain goat. In July 2007, thirty **Townsend's big-eared bats** were observed emerging from Stanton's Cave, indicating that it is still an active bat colony habitat. In 1997, the cave entrance was outfitted with bat-friendly gating to protect this bat that is of special concern in Arizona.

Grand Canyoneering: Grand Canyon Caverns is located outside Grand Canyon National Park along historic Route 66 west of the South Rim, in the vicinity of Peach Springs, Arizona. The caverns are a privately owned enterprise discovered by prospector Walter Peck in 1927. Hoping for gold and silver strikes, Peck had ore from the caverns assayed in Prescott, Arizona. No gold or silver were found, but Peck discovered he could sell the caverns as a tourist destination. For 25 cents, from 1927 to 1935, guests were lowered down the 210 feet to the main floor of the cavern by rope and lantern. In 1936, Hoover Dam engineers were influenced to improve the cavern entrance, and they built a staircase. In 1962, an elevator was installed. Subsequently, it was discovered—by deploying smoke bombs—that the air supply to the cavern originates from Havasu Falls on the Havasupai Indian Reservation, approximately 60 miles distant.

Angels Window is located 8 aerial miles southeast of the North Rim's Grand Canyon Lodge at an elevation of 7,820 feet. Angels Window is an approximately 100-foot tall by 80-foot wide triangle-shaped erosion opening in the North Rim's Cape Royal. **Angels Window Overlook** along the Cape Royal Road provides a broadside view of the window and through it a view of the Colorado River. From the Colorado River, Angels Widow can be seen from the Unkar Creek Delta.

Uplifting. Angels Window at Cape Royal, North Rim, 1937. GRCA 496

Alamo Window is located in Fern Glen Canyon, 46 aerial miles northwest of the North Rim's Grand Canyon Lodge. The window has a 60-foot opening.

Cheops Window is located in the Cheops Pyramid formation, 6 aerial miles southwest of the North Rim's Grand Canyon Lodge, at an elevation of 5,350 feet. Backpacker Harvey Butchart notes that Cheops Window is a 15-foot by 15-foot broken rock outcropping at the top of the north buttress.

The Bridge of Sighs is located at Colorado River mile 35.6 in the Marble Canyon section of Grand Canyon. In 1911, the bridge was discovered and named by the Kolb Brothers, Ellsworth and Emery, while traveling the river to film their journey. This is the only known natural bridge that can be seen from river level. Ellsworth named the Bridge of Sighs for Antonio Contino's bridge in Venice, Italy, constructed in 1600. Lord Byron helped to popularize the belief that the bridge's name was inspired by the sighs of condemned prisoners as they were led over it to the executioner. In reality, the days of summary executions were over by the time the bridge was built.

Fallen Tower Bridge is located in the Eminence Break formations 31 aerial miles northeast of the South Rim's El Tovar Hotel. Backcountry hiker, Harvey Butchart, notes that the bridge is a small-scale pinnacle that fell from a balanced rock position 100 feet below the rim of the Kaibab Limestone Formation. The rock became lodged in place across a 30-foot wide ravine.

Hartman Natural Bridge is located 7 aerial miles east of the North Rim's Grand Canyon Lodge in the north arm of Lava Canyon. The bridge is 130 feet by just under 130 feet and is named for discoverer James Hartman.

Ranger Station:

How many caves are in the Grand Canyon? Recorded to date, there are 335 caves that feature spectacular mineral formations, such as stalactites and stalagmites. These and other formations, called "speleothems," are significant to the study of caves. Speleothems indicate drought and non-drought conditions. The amount of growth of such formations may be a gauge to how much, or how little, ground water seeped into and dripped onto a cave floor.

Concealed by the Inner Canyon topography, the National Park Service estimates that 700 caves are yet to be discovered in Grand Canyon.

Ranger Station:

What is the largest natural bridge in the canyon? Kolb Natural Bridge has the largest span, being 147 feet long. It is located below the North Rim's Point Imperial. The bridge formed at the crest of a cliff, where a seasonal tributary stream originates and flows over the rim to Nankoweap Creek. Fissures in the rock allowed the creek to undercut the crest and excavate a new path, leaving a horizontal arched span between the two banks of the stream. The bridge left behind, having been formed by a waterfall, is called a waterfall natural bridge.

Ranger Station:

What's the difference between a geologic window and a geologic arch? Windows measure less than 3' x 3,' and arches measure greater than 3' x3'. Angels Window, on the North Rim at Cape Royal, is far larger than 3'x3' and was descriptively named for its broadside view toward the heavens.

Keyhole Natural Bridge is located 33 aerial miles northwest of the South Rim's El Tovar Hotel in the 140 Mile Canyon. The bridge was discovered by P.T. Reilly from his self-made aerial photo.

Kolb Natural Bridge is located 8 aerial miles northeast of the North Rim's Grand Canyon Lodge at an elevation of 7,040 feet. The natural bridge was confirmed aerially by Barry Goldwater in 1951. Goldwater initiated the naming of the feature with the Department of the Interior in honor of Emery Kolb. Backcountry hiker, Harvey Butchart, has said that its undocumented discovery was by George and Charles McCormick as they combed the area for the gold they believed was hidden by John Doyle Lee.

Royal Arch is located 19 aerial miles northwest of the South Rim's El Tovar Hotel at an elevation of 3,200 feet. The arch is 60 feet high and 60 feet wide and has a 40-foot-deep passage. This is the only known arch in Grand Canyon National Park to have a year-round flowing stream, **Royal Arch Creek,** passing through it. **Royal Arch Falls** is 150 feet beyond the arch. The creek ultimately reaches the Colorado River at Elves Chasm.

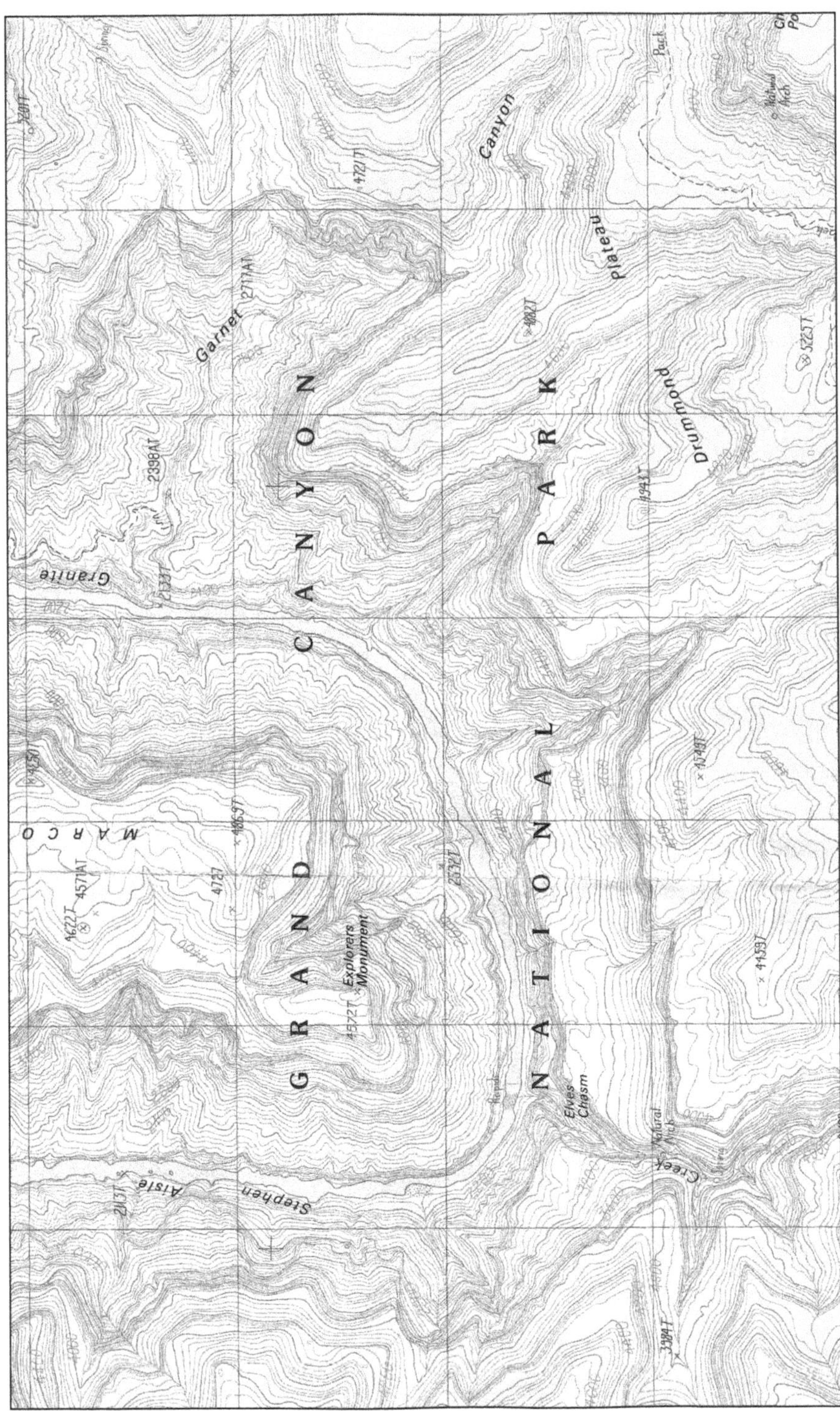

Elves Chasm and Royal Arch, Inner Canyon. USGS 7.5 minute series *Explorers Monument*

Life in the Grand Canyon

Amphibians found in the Grand Canyon include the canyon tree frog, tiger salamander (two slightly differing subspecies: Arizona tiger salamander and Utah tiger salamander), Rocky Mountain toad, Great Basin spade-foot toad (lives in burrows much of the year), leopard frog (rare in the Colorado River corridor, and are known to exist at only a few sites), red-spotted toad, and the western spade-foot frog.

Grand Canyoneering: The strata fossil record includes: mollusks (invertebrates having a soft unsegmented body, usually shell-enclosed), brachiopods (mollusk-like shellfish having a pair of arms bearing tentacles to capture food), worms, snails, clams, trilobites, primitive fresh water fish, fish teeth, petrified sea floor ripples and mud cracks, sea lilies, reptile and amphibian tracks (termed trace fossils), conifers, ferns, and raindrop impressions.

Fossilized. Trilobite, 1930. GRCA 5678

Insects and spiders include honey bees, black flies, wasps, tarantula hawks, beetles, black ants, wood spiders, garden spiders, black widow spiders, and tarantulas. At and near river level and along side streams, many species of spiders and several species of scorpions can be found, including the bark scorpion and the giant hairy scorpion that inhabit the Colorado River corridor. Scorpions have two pincers and an elongated tail with a stinger tip. Feeding at night, scorpions have two eyes on the center of the head and typically two to five eyes along the perimeter. Riparian, or "stream-side," scorpions that reside under rocks or tree bark usually carry their tails to one side, while scorpions that live in burrows hold their tails upwards.

Butterflies found in the Grand Canyon include the alfalfa, Arizona's sister, Baird's swallowtail, Colorado hairstreak, Grand Canyon ringlet, Ingham's orange-tip monarch, Mormon metalmark, mourning cloak, Nevada skipper, Satyr, Schellbach's fritillary, silver-spotted skipper, snout, Weidemeyer's admiral, west coast lady, western tiger swallowtail, and the yucca skipper.

Birds found in the Grand Canyon depend on season, breeding habits, and other conditions such as migratory ranges. Of the 355 species of birds recorded at Grand Canyon, included are: acorn woodpecker, bald eagle, black-chinned hummingbird, black-crowned night heron, California condor, Cooper's hawk, golden eagle, goshawk, great blue heron, great horned owl, Mexican spotted owl, northern oriole, peregrine falcon, raven, red-tailed hawk, road runner, screech owl, turkey, turkey vulture, Virginia's warbler, Steller's jay, and the white-throated swift.

California condors were reintroduced to the Grand Canyon in an effort of species survival. Grand Canyon was chosen because the National Park's remote and rugged terrain best protected the bird. Condors formerly ranged the North American continent from Canada to Mexico and are the largest land birds in North America. Adult birds weigh up to 20 pounds and have a wingspan of 9.5 feet, which enables the bird to soar thermal air currents for hours and travel 200 miles per day. In 1924, the last confirmed northern Arizona sighting was 60 miles south of Grand Canyon near Williams, Arizona. By 1982, the condor population declined to 22. An intrepid captivity endeavor of remaining condors was conducted to save the species from extinction. Breeding programs began bird preservation at San Diego Wild Animal Park in California. In the species recovery effort in 1996, the Peregrine Fund and the United States Fish and Wildlife Service with two male and four female birds performed a condor release 30 miles north of the Grand Canyon's Marble Canyon at the Vermilion Cliffs region of the Arizona Strip. Condors are now reproducing again in the wild. Arizona Game and Fish Department director Duane Shroufe said, *This is truly what wildlife reintroduction is all about—natural reproduction in the wild. This is wildlife history in the making.* Today, condors soar the Grand Canyon skies

> **Grand Canyoneering:** The Vermilion Cliffs are located north of the Grand Canyon's Marble Canyon boundary. The 3,000-foot-high Moenkopi Sandstone Formation feature makes up a fraction of the 110,000-acre *Paria Canyon–Vermilion Cliff* geographic unit of the Arizona Strip region. This rugged territory, though not a section of the National Park, demonstrates itself as a wilderness buffer to Grand Canyon. Forming House Rock Valley at the base of the cliffs and the horizon line as seen from North Rim overlooks, such as Point Imperial, the Vermilion Cliffs were used for the first time in 1996 as the California condor reintroduction site.

One-story wing span. California condor, Grand Canyon Village, South Rim. GRCA D0511

Grand Canyoneering: The Mexican spotted owl has a round head and dark eyes. The adult owl is 16 to 19 inches long with a dark brown body with white spots and brown barring. The most common "call" is two to three short hoots followed by a prolonged hoot. Describing the Grand Canyon environment perfectly, the owl typically roosts and breeds in deep canyons or in diverse forested habitats. Nesting is usually in a rugged canyon recess or cave, or in abandoned nests. The Mexican spotted owl lays one to three white eggs between the months of April and May with an incubation of approximately 30 days. The owl is regarded as a great rodent eater. Active only at night, the owl generally feeds on medium sized mammals with the most common and important item being the woodrat, depending on availability.

and, because they are a curious bird, are partial to the South Rim's Grand Canyon Village. Beginning in 2006, observers documented several active nesting sites. Today's population: nearly 400, of which about 70 reside at Grand Canyon.

The presence of the Mexican spotted owl at Grand Canyon was confirmed in 1992, and it was listed as a threatened species in 1993. Like the locales of other biological recovery efforts, the Grand Canyon is an ideal habitat for a recovery program because of the remote and inaccessible rugged terrain. Owl population surveys were conducted in 1994 and 1995 along the North Rim, and the results highlighted the need for a recovery program. Critical habitat, which comprises most of Grand Canyon National Park, was established in 2001. On the Colorado Plateau, in general, the owl is likely threatened by impacts of overgrazing, road building, and recreation. In Grand Canyon National Park specifically, the owl is threatened by cataclysmic wildfire, and in the surrounding Kaibab National Forest by wildfire and timber harvests. Back in 1977, the National Audubon Society recognized that the condition of the Mexican spotted owl required continued study to determine what additional protection it needed, apart from that which shelters all owls.

Mammals found in Grand Canyon include desert bighorn sheep, mule deer, elk, black bear, mountain lion, badger, bobcat, coyote, fox, raccoon, spotted and striped skunk, beaver, muskrats, river otter (may have disappeared from the park in the last ten years), mice, rats, shrews, squirrels, and cacomistle—also called ringtail and miner's cat. Twenty species of bats have been reported in Grand Canyon, including the Arizona, big brown, Townsend's big-eared, Mex-

Cooling system advanced. Desert bighorn sheep utilize Inner Canyon thermals to regulate body temperature. GRCA D3939

ican free-tailed, and the western pipistrelle, which is the bat most common to the observer as they are seen feeding on insects from sundown to sunrise.

Mule deer on the Kaibab Plateau in the early 1900s were protected from predator animals to promote the region as a hunter's destination. Primarily, mountain lions, bobcats, wolves, and coyotes were systematically hunted on the North Rim. As a result, the deer population that once naturally numbered at approximately 4,000 proliferated unchecked and grew to an astounding 50,000 to 100,000. By 1924, the plateau's ecological balance had collapsed. That winter, with all possible forage consumed, including lower tree branches, thousands of deer died of starvation. In the aftermath, rehabilitation programs went into effect to correct and recover the deer herds. Even though hunting predator animals was negated in Grand Canyon National Park, the surrounding area did not have the same restrictions.

Grand Canyoneering: California condors and other wildlife, such as the Mexican spotted owl, are protected under the *Endangered Species Act*, which provides for all wildlife and plants in serious peril. The act also calls for the conservation of the land, water, and airspace, called **critical habitat**, which an endangered species needs for survival. This includes breeding sites and surrounding environment that give room for normal population growth and behavior.

The Kaibab squirrel is the tassel-eared squirrel that was separated from its relative, the Abert's squirrel, by conditions of the Grand Canyon's chasm development and elevation change. The Kaibab squirrel has a 20-mile by 40-mile habitat confined to the ponderosa pine forest of the North Rim of Grand Canyon National Park and the northern section of the Kaibab National Forest, in the vicinity of Jacob Lake, Arizona. The Kaibab squirrel is 19 to 21 inches long, weighs up to 2 pounds, and is named after its isolation to the North Rim's Kaibab Plateau. Over time, the squirrel developed a black-dark gray body and a unique white tail. The squirrel prefers to feed primarily on the tender under-bark of the ponderosa pine and greatly enjoys truffles—the fungus that resembles a rough-skinned potato. In 1965, 200,000 acres within the Grand Canyon National Park and the Kaibab National Forest were declared the Kaibab Squirrel National Natural Landmark. The program recognizes and encourages the conservation of outstanding examples of the United States' natural history. Under the authority of the Historic Sites Act of 1935, and administered by the National Park Service, the National Natural Landmark program was established on May 18, 1962, by United States Secretary of the Interior Stewart Udall.

Fish native to the Colorado River in Grand Canyon include the bluehead sucker, bonytail chub, Colorado pikeminnow (formerly Colorado Squawfish), flannelmouth sucker, humpback chub, razorback sucker, roundtail chub, and the

Grand Canyoneering: Biological soil crust, also known as cryptogamic soil, cryptobiotic soil, microphytic and microbiotic crusts, are microscopic non-vascular assemblages composed of nitrogen-rich blue-green algae, diatoms, brown algae, lichens, and mosses. Biological crusts grow on and within soils and make important modifications to the layers that they occupy. The crusts heighten the nutrient content of the soil and slow the erosion process. The crusts also help to retain soil moisture. These delicate mat-like features sustain seeds that mature into plant communities. Disturbing this environment can tear down decades of growth and development. Found elsewhere in the canyon as well, the Esplanade Formation is a primary host environment.

speckled dace. The construction of Glen Canyon Dam has resulted in an environmentally changed Colorado River in Grand Canyon. The changes include not only a colder river with a greatly reduced sediment content (the native fish are accustomed to a warmer muddy river), but the dam also permanently interrupted the instinctual migratory habits and range of the fish—they were uprooted—extirpated. The humpback chub school can be found primarily at the confluence of the Little Colorado River and Colorado River in the Grand Canyon, where the natively warmer Little Colorado boosts the water temperature of the surrounding mainstream Colorado. In 1978, the National Park Service placed an off-limits to fishing restriction at the mouth of the Little Colorado River, which includes the mainstream Colorado River for .5 mile, up and downstream, to save and preserve this hatchery site. Nonnative fish such as trout, catfish, and carp added to the demise of the native fish. Carp feed on eggs and disturb breeding habitats, and catfish voraciously feed on fish larvae.

Reptiles found in the Grand Canyon include the Gila monster, western desert banded gecko, western collard lizard, California king snake, gopher snake, and the desert tortoise (rare). Six rattlesnake species have been documented in the park and include the southwestern speckled rattlesnake and the northern black-tailed rattlesnake. Both of these are rarely seen. The other four are subspecies of the western diamondback: Hopi rattlesnake, Mojave rattlesnake, Great Basin rattlesnake, and the most common, the pink-colored Grand Canyon rattlesnake.

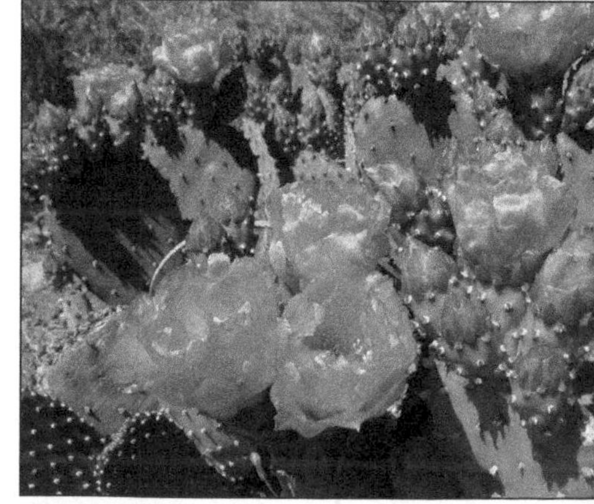

Spine tingling blooms. Prickly pear cactus, Inner Canyon. GRCA D3206

Wildflower varieties number approximately 650 at Grand Canyon National Park. Some of the common species that display a **white flower** include the night blooming **sacred datura.** While this plant has a most beautiful bloom, the whole plant is poisonous, containing several alkaloids—most notably, *atropine*. Humans, as well as horses and cattle, have been poisoned and occasionally killed from consuming this plant. **Evening primrose** is another white flower of the night, relying on night-flying insects to pollinate the fragrant blossoms. The **sego lily** is commonly seen in bloom in the forests of both the North and South Rims in the summer. In times of food scarcity in the past, the bulbs were eaten by both the Navajo (Diné) and the Hopi Indians, as well as pioneers traveling into Utah. **Cliffrose** has fragrant cream-colored flowers. The pealed bark was used by Native Americans to make sandals, mats, and rope. The Navajo and the Hopi used the wood from the shrub to make arrows.

Yellow flowers include the **Utah agave,** which is one of the most widely dispersed plants in the park. It has established itself on both the North Rim and South Rim and in all the life zones, in some of the most rocky and hot locations, down to the Colorado River. The Utah agave is often called a century plant because it takes many years for the flowering stalk to appear. The actual life span is fifteen to twenty-five years. When it is ready to extend its stalk, the process is rapid—about four to six inches per day. Early Native Americans of the Inner Canyon roasted agaves for food in "agave ovens" or "mescal pits." This term *mescal* comes from the Spanish name for agave. **Western wallflower** is of the mustard family and blooms almost half of the year, from April along the Tonto Plateau to August on the North Rim. These are an admired yellow-orange flower found in Grand Canyon Village and along the Hermit Road and the Desert View–East Rim Drive. Native Americans used the plant material for medicinal purposes, including the treatment of sunburn. The **Wright's and Utah deervetch** flower from June to September. The Utah species is common to the North Rim and the Wright's to the South Rim. It is browsed by deer, giving it its common name. The Wright's species was used by the Navajo to heal wounds and to relieve digestive disorders. **Hairy gold-aster** blooms from June to September. The showy herb is found on the North Rim at Greenland Lake and Cape Royal and on the South Rim in Grand Canyon Village, along the Hermit Road, and in the upper elevations of the Inner Canyon. Hopi Indians used the leaves to make a tea.

Red flowers include **globemallow,** of which there are approximately nine species. As a testimony to C. Hart Merriam's Life Zone definition, different species of globemallow inhabit different elevations between the rims of the canyon and the Colorado River. The Hopi Indians used the stems of the plant as a form of chewing gum. The plant is also browsed on by the desert bighorn sheep. **Early Indian and Wyoming paintbrush** are the two most widespread of the four common species of paintbrush. While the two species overlap in their distribution, Early Indian paintbrush is typical to the Inner Canyon and Wyoming paintbrush is found on the North Rim, abundantly along the Cape Royal Road, and on the

South Rim along the Desert View–East Rim Drive. Hopi Indians ate the flowers raw and used them in ceremonies. **Crimson monkeyflower** is one of six species of *Mimulus cardinalis* documented in Grand Canyon National Park. The plant occurs where there are large shady seeps, springs, and creeks such as Bright Angel Creek at Phantom Ranch and at remote regions such as Elves Chasm.

Pink flowers include **trailing four-o'clock windmills,** which bloom between the Tonto Plateau and the Colorado River from spring through summer and endure into fall. The flowers open at dawn and stay open for several hours in areas such as Indian Garden, Phantom Ranch, and Ribbon Falls until they succumb to the heat of the Inner Canyon. **Rocky Mountain beeplant** blooms in late summer, particularly near the Grand Canyon Depot. The abundance of this flower relies on the frequency of summer thunderstorms—or monsoons.

Blue flowers include the **Rocky Mountain iris,** which blooms in early summer and favors the meadows of the North Rim. **Lupine,** of which nine species have been documented in Grand Canyon National Park, are found on the North Rim and the South Rim—especially along the roadsides, where the plants are incubated. The pavement provides radiating warmth and delivers shed rain water and snowmelt down to the road's shoulders.

Grand Canyoneering: The African burro was used by miners of the late 1800s and early 1900s to haul supplies and ore. Some of the burros roamed the canyon and multiplied, ensuring the miners of a steady stock supply. As mining claims were abandoned, the burros continued to multiply. The ecosystem became threatened as the trails of the growing numbers of burros eroded the terrain. Additionally, the accelerated plant consumption by the increased numbers of burros left too little forage for the native mule deer and desert bighorn sheep. An environmental restoration program began in 1924 initiating the removal of the burros.

Net gain. Capturing feral burros with helicopter "sling load" cargo mesh, ca 1974. GRCA 6630

Trees found in the Grand Canyon include bigtooth maple, Rocky Mountain maple, Gambel oak, quaking aspen, pinyon pine, Utah juniper, ponderosa pine, Douglas fir, blue spruce, Engelmann spruce, and Fremont cottonwood.

The seeds of pinyon pine, also called "pine nuts," were a primary food source for the Native Americans. The seed of the pine cone was eaten raw, roasted, or ground into a meal. The tufts of needles were used for a tea, and the inner bark provided food in lean years. The trunks and limbs were used for lumber. Native

Americans used the modified pine cone, or "berry," of the Utah Juniper as a meat seasoning. The cones were also cooked or eaten raw. The acorns of the Gambel oak were ground into a meal. Bark of the quaking aspen served as a fever reducer.

Grand Canyoneering: Mountain lions typically use the rim's plateaus for range and utilize the canyon's upper ledges for resting. Sometimes their travels are astounding. A GPS-collared female lion descended from the South Rim and without delay swam across the 300-foot-wide Colorado River. She then ascended to the North Rim, where her collar was lost and she could be tracked no further. All in just eight hours.

Shrubs found in the Grand Canyon include antelope brush, Apache plume, canyon grape, corkbark, fir, desert thorn, greasebush, New Mexican locust, western rosebud, sagebrush, hackberry, Utah serviceberry, blackbrush, four-wing saltbush, rubber rabbitbrush, mesquite, cliffrose, greenleaf manzanita, and mountain mahogany.

The stems of Apache plume were used by some Native American tribes as arrow shafts. The Hopi used the New Mexican locust to treat symptoms of arthritis. The berries of Utah serviceberry were milled and formed into a sweet hard loaf that could be rehydrated and added to other foods. Branches of cliffrose were used by the Hopi and Navajo for arrow shafts. The Hopi also used the plant for cleansing injuries. Tea and chewing gum were made from the ground bark and wood of rubber rabbitbrush.

Ranger Station:
How are bat colonies accounted for in the canyon? For harmless bat capture and identification, a fine gauge diamond mesh called a "mist net" is installed in the flight paths near certain known bat roost areas, such as Phantom Ranch. The nets are extremely lightweight. An 8' x 30' net weighs in at only four ounces. The key to safe observation is that a qualified person is always present to quickly release captured bats.

Ranger Station:
I heard some deer were shot by park rangers. Why is that? Twenty-two deer were humanly shot to death by rangers at the Phantom Ranch-Bright Angel Campground area at the bottom of the canyon. Even though area deer were browsing, they were experiencing slow, horrible deaths by starvation. In addition to browsing, the deer were consuming human food and the plastic bags and foil wrappers used to contain the food.

After performing autopsies on the deer, wildlife biologists discovered up to five pounds of trash clogging the deer's stomachs and intestines, which inhibited nourishment from deer's natural browse.

Cactus found in the Grand Canyon include barrel, beavertail, claretcup, cottoncup, Engelmann's hedgehog and prickly pear, pincushion, plains prickly pear, Simpson's hedgehog, and Whipple cholla.

The Hopi Indians boiled the pulpy yellow fruits of the Whipple cholla and ate them with squash. The edible purplish fruit of prickly pear can be eaten raw or cooked to make jams. The seeds of beavertail form a vital link in the local food chain, as the seeds are eaten by rodents.

Grand Canyon Affected by Dams

Buck Farm Canyon, located 16 aerial miles northeast of the North Rim's Grand Canyon Lodge in Marble Canyon, was an early Hoover Dam site considered by the Bureau of Reclamation.

Grand Canyoneering: When dams were studied for feasibility in Marble Canyon, Bureau of Reclamation crews reached Marble Canyon's South Rim by cutting a 25-mile long road from Cedar Ridge, Arizona, through Navajo Indian Reservation land. To study this site from the rim at Tatahatso Point, located 29 aerial miles northeast of the South Rim's El Tovar Hotel and at an elevation of 5,702 feet, a toe-hold descent was made down to the Colorado River.

Shortly after, a 20-foot-high tower was positioned on the rim, and a 3,667-foot-long tram cable was installed. The cableway ran from the rim to the opposite side of the canyon, where it was anchored on the north bank of the river. A one-way trip took up to 14 minutes to complete. Under the Department of the Interior, the goals of the Bureau of Reclamation are to protect, manage, and develop water resources of the United States. *Reclamation* is "to bring 'wasteland,' or land that was formerly underwater, under cultivation."

The Hoover Dam, in relation to Grand Canyon National Park, created the downstream Lake Mead, which in turn backed up the Colorado River into the western canyon region—in effect "pooling," or covering, many of the last Grand Canyon rapids. Negatively affecting the native fish, such as the Colorado squawfish, the dam closed the downstream migration habitat in the lower Colorado River, while Glen Canyon Dam later closed off the upstream migration habitat. Hoover Dam, also known as the Boulder Canyon Project, began in 1935 when the Colorado River was diverted at the construction site. The dam produces hydroelectric power and also serves as an irrigation regulator. Cost: $175,000,000; height: 726 feet; crest span: 1,244 feet; crest width: 45 feet; base span: 600 feet; base width: 660 feet; concrete: 7,000,000 tons. **Lake Mead** is named for Elwood Mead who assertively promoted nationwide water conservation projects. The 9.7 trillion gallon lake begins at the Grand Wash Cliffs and floods 40 miles of the western Grand Canyon. The lake has a 250-square-mile surface area and 550 miles of shoreline.

Colonel Claude Birdseye led the 1923, 3-month long, United States Geological Survey in the Grand Canyon and vicinity to locate feasible dam sites in the canyon. Birdseye located twenty-one sites utilizing field notes from Major John Wesley Powell, Frederick Dellenbaugh, of Powell's second river expedition, and the Kolb Brothers. There were five exploration boats, the *Marble*, *Glen*, *Grand*, *Boulder*, and *Mojave*. Equipment included a radio transceiver that was set up on shore and enabled the crew to learn of President Warren Harding's death in San Francisco, California.

Bright Angel Dam was proposed in 1907 by the Boston, Massachusetts, firm of Warner, Tucker, and Company. The partnership desired to build a hydroelectric dam in the Grand Canyon's Granite Gorge at the bottom of the Bright Angel Trail at Pipe Creek. The design called for a 600-foot-high dam that would create a 15-mile long lake. The plan failed due to a lack of financial support.

Dams studied for feasibility in Marble Canyon brought such groups as the Sierra Club in vigorous opposition in 1956. Studies were done to determine if a hydroelectric, tandem dam system located seven miles apart within the narrow canyon section would be effective energy producers. The sites were partially examined by helicopter as pilot Lynn Roberts ferried surveyors to the Colorado River. It was at this time that Roberts also flew archaeologist Dr. Robert Euler in the vicinity to search for and recover site artifacts that would become submerged if dams were constructed. In 1975, the Bureau of Reclamation waived the endeavor when Marble Canyon National Monument gained National Park status under the authority of President Gerald Ford.

Grand Canyoneering: In the winter of 1982–83, a heavy snowfall occurred that would later create an unstoppable heavy river flow into Lake Powell and would consequently stage the near failure of Glen Canyon Dam.

In the events leading up to June 1983, engineers attempted to reduce the level of Lake Powell by running the dam's eight generators at full capacity, and by opening the dam's four river outlet tubes in an attempt to reconcile the water that was rushing in. However, inflow forecasts anticipated that this procedure would not be enough to reduce the volume of the reservoir to accommodate the snowmelt. The spillways at each side of the dam would have to be used. Alarmingly, as the spillways opened up, the white water charging out of one of the passages became dark with Navajo sandstone rocks, and then, boulders. The water, pushing through the spillway, was causing vacuum pockets over the rough surface of the concrete lining. The dam was in jeopardy. Rapidly, the spillway was disintegrating. The geological mechanics of erosion were beginning.

In a last ditch effort to prevent the failure of Glen Canyon Dam, the flow through the spillways was greatly reduced and plywood was added to the top of the dam at the spillway gates to curb the lake water at the crest. Had the water overflowed the dam, in zipper-like action, there would have been a peeling effect as the concrete dam eroded.

Glen Canyon Dam at Page, Arizona, is managed by the Bureau of Reclamation and the Western Area Power Administration to provide hydroelectric power to seven western states. The site is 20 river miles upstream from Grand Canyon National Park's eastern boundary line. Using 5,370,000 cubic yards of concrete, the dam is 710 feet tall, 1,560 feet long and 25 feet wide at the crest, and 300 feet wide at the base. Final project cost: $215,000,000. President Dwight D. Eisenhower

UFO site? In 1968, three years after this photo was taken, 20th Century Fox would "crash land" the spaceship *Icarus* in Lake Powell's Padre Bay in Pierre Boulle's *Planet of the Apes.*

Silent trumpet. Glen Canyon Dam and Lake Powell still in their infancy, 1965. GRCA 9708

activated the first dynamite blast from Washington D.C. in 1956, which began the construction of Glen Canyon Dam. **Lake Powell** is named for Major John Wesley Powell. The 9 trillion gallon Lake Powell has 1,960 miles of shoreline and floods nearly 100 large side canyons that are predominantly in Utah.

The Glen Canyon Dam Beach/Habitat Building Flow began in 1996 in the hope of simulating a flood-like condition to stir up sediment that has made it into

Grand Canyoneering: A Glen Canyon Dam *forebay dam*, a voluminous water retention zone, was proposed by the Bureau of Reclamation. Though not approved, this secondary dam was suggested to "eliminate" beach-stripping along the Colorado River in Grand Canyon. As proposed, a forebay dam would seize the "peak operation" rush of water as it exits Glen Canyon Dam's electricity generating system. Once in this holding area, the water would be released gradually into the Grand Canyon ecosystem. In theory, Grand Canyon beaches may have stabilized. However, had the project gone through, the remaining 15 westerly miles of Glen Canyon would have been flooded.

the canyon on the downstream side of Glen Canyon Dam. The objective is to send sand down to the beaches that have been in the erosion mode since the completion of the dam. An elevated push of water theoretically would redistribute the material. The historic floods that formerly entered the Grand Canyon came by way of Glen Canyon and other upstream sites such as the San Juan River. Today, the dam impounds the sediment. The water that passes through Glen Canyon Dam is virtually sediment free and is the eroding force of the existing sandbars and deltas. Side canyons below the dam, such as the Paria River, the Little Colorado River, and the Kanab Creek, are the principal contributors of sand and other natural material to the river channel for which this "flooding program" hopes to distribute. Results: beaches and sandbars were reestablished. However, erosion resumed within six months.

Lava Dam remnants on the canyon walls in western Grand Canyon disclose a series of lava flows that once originated from the area of the Pine Mountains. In this area called Toroweap, one such flow proceeded 84 miles downstream, following the Colorado River channel. Historically, Prospect and Toroweap Dams blocked the river at mile 179, which formed lakes. Eventually the dams were breeched by the river and eroded.

Ranger Station:

What happened to the Grand Canyon and the Colorado River during the filling of Lake Mead and Lake Powell? The lengthy ecosystem damage occurred twice—at Lake Mead in the 1930s and at Lake Powell from 1963 to 1980. During the years of lake filling, the Colorado River Delta at the Gulf of California, of the greater geologic region called the Salton Trough, received virtually no fresh water and renewing silt. The region was devastated by dehydration.

Lake Powell was filled as quickly as possible. The only consideration was the need for a sufficient reservoir to drive the power generators in Hoover Dam downstream. When the floodgates closed at Glen Canyon Dam in 1963, the Colorado River was allowed to pass through the canyon for two years at the greatly reduced rate of 25 percent in order to jumpstart the filling of Lake Powell.

Immediately in 1963, the river began to flow predictably through the Inner Canyon and the annual floods needed to carry material for the rejuvenation of beaches passed away behind the dam, buried under Lake Powell. The Grand Canyon was forever changed as the river and canyon began their adjustment to the blockage at Glen Canyon.

Ranger Station:

How does Glen Canyon Dam stay in place? Glen Canyon Dam is an arch-gravity dam. Its 10 million tons of concrete bows upstream, wedged in against the Navajo Sandstone canyon walls by the pressure of the nine trillion gallons of water in Lake Powell. Instead of the Colorado River—now a massive lake—moving the obstruction out of the way, the river unwittingly works together with the dam to keep it from toppling downstream.

Ranger Station:

How big were the lava dams at Toroweap? Lava flowing from the canyon rim area created a natural dam over 200 feet high, which flooded the Inner Canyon wilderness with a lake some 40 miles long.

Called the Toroweap Cascade Event, geologist estimate that several natural dams occupied the area, with the most recent occurring some 140,000 years ago.

Trans-Canyon Water Line

Del Rio and Bellemont, Arizona, were the historic sites where railroad tank cars were filled with water for delivery to the South Rim. The Trans-Canyon Water Line brought an end to this method of water management.

Grand Canyoneering: On the South Rim's massive Coconino Plateau region, there are a variety of over forty historic *tanks* for water storage. Because surface water is regionally rare, this method of water retrieval and storage continues today on the North and South Rims. Modern and archaic methods of saving water are utilized in the form of *catchments,* which are excavated U-shaped earthen embankments or steel containers with a sieve—also called a *trick tank.*

Built in 1925, the derelict Pasture Wash Ranger Station, located 15 aerial miles northwest of the South Rim's Grand Canyon Village, has an advanced trick tank system. At an elevation of 6,296 feet, the station's sloped roof is outfitted with an eaves long trough. The trough channels rain and snowmelt to a down spout that is fixed at the lower end to a holding tank fashioned with a spigot.

The Verkamp's Curios shop is equipped with an advanced system located under the front porch and was still in use into the 1970s.

In the 1890s, the Grand View Hotel was outfitted with a cunning trough network that conformed to the trailing edge of the multi-gabled roof line. The water then traveled to a holding tank.

Demand for supply. Unloading water from tank cars for domestic use at the South Rim, 1961. GRCA 3605

Left: **Archaic water storage.** Catchment system in a meadow on the North Rim, 1934. This style still in use today. GRCA 9167

Above: **In its heyday.** Pasture Wash Ranger Station served as a shelter for ranger patrols, South Rim near Bass Camp, 1936. Fallen to dilapidation, restoration has begun. GRCA 1033

The Trans-Canyon Water Line is the water system that delivers all potable water to the Grand Canyon's South and North Rims. Due to water allocations in the states that the Colorado River supplies with water, it could not be used for Grand Canyon's metropolitan districts, as Arizona's allotment had already been established. Using state-of-the-art techniques and overcoming major obstacles, crews completed the water line in 1970. The completed project brought an end to the historic water shortage at Grand Canyon. Before the construction of the water line, all water was delivered by train and truck. Contractor Elling Halvorson said of the project, *The line is 13.5 miles long. It is the 'crookedest' water line with approximately 195 vertical and hundreds of horizontal bends. The* [aluminum pipe] *line was welded together. All joints were x-rayed in the field. This is the largest helicopter-supported project to have ever been done in the United States.* During construction in 1964, a forest fire in Roaring Springs Canyon melted the aluminum pipeline, and in 1966, a flash flood destroyed 8.5 miles of the pipeline. Breaks in the pipeline still occur today. Typically caused by the cool nights and hot days, breaks will take place due to the expanding and contracting of the aluminum—like bending a coat hanger back-and-forth until it breaks. To repair a break, that section of pipe is cut out and flown from the Inner Canyon and used as a model to fabricate a new section. The new piece is installed at the same time of day as when the damaged piece was removed. Because temperature differences can be so extreme, a three-inch expansion or contraction size difference can take place.

> **Grand Canyoneering:** The Indian Garden Water Line was installed in 1931, prior to the Trans-Canyon Water Line, which was completed in 1970. A pumping station was installed and a 6-inch-diameter pipe was laid. By 1932, the modern era of water management relieved the need for water delivery by railroad tank cars from Del Rio and Bellemont, Arizona.

A modern Roaring Springs pumping station was constructed in 1979, which elevates the spring water 3,539 feet to the North Rim, where three discretely placed water holding tanks have a combined capacity of 4 million gallons. Prior to 1928, when

Water shed. Roaring Springs Pumphouse. Notice the helipad (right), ca 1980. GRCA 18932

Elusive storage. South Rim water tanks can only be seen from the air, ca 1980. GRCA 18823

the spring was made inaccessible by a rock slide, the North Rim received water from Bright Angel Spring, located in the Transept, a side canyon west of Grand Canyon Lodge. In 1928, Roaring Springs became the North Rim's water and power source. Supported by the Union Pacific Railroad, the Utah Parks Company placed a pump station, dam, and power plant, long since removed, at the confluence of Bright Angel Creek and Roaring Springs Creek.

The spring water flows southerly in the Trans-Canyon Water Line. By gravity, the water flows under the North Kaibab Trail and under the Silver Suspension Bridge, for which the bridge was made, and over the Colorado River where it reaches the pumping station at Indian Garden. The water is then "pushed" to the discretely placed South Rim holding tanks, which have a combined capacity of 13 million gallons.

Ranger Station:

How many passengers fly the canyon via Papillon Grand Canyon Helicopters? They fly 170,000 passengers annually.

Snow

Snow on the North Rim ranges from 120 to more than 200 inches of accumulation annually. The North Rim remains open year-around. However, visitor services are only open from mid-May to mid-October. Frequently, Arizona State Highway 67 closes due to heavy snow or drifts, but entry to the park technically remains open. Winter visitors to the North Rim must be able and equipped to handle mountain climates and be ready to depart the rim area should the weather shift beyond their ability to cope. A **winter fence** is a snow drift at high elevation that blocks access to the North Rim.

Regaining the road. Snow plow on the South Rim, 1931. GRCA 106

Snow on the South Rim annually averages 6 to 10 inches of accumulation, but has the potential to receive enough snow to be measured by the foot. South Rim visitor services remain open year-around.

A snowmobile route was created utilizing a series of Forest Service Roads. The 80-mile-long round trip course travels from Jacob Lake, Arizona, to the North Rim's Timp Point at the elevation of 7,508 feet.

Ranger Station:

How do hikers keep from slipping on the icy trails in the winter, especially while carrying a loaded backpack? Hikers attach crampons to the bottom of their boots. There are several versions, including a full crampon (typically provides twelve sharp points of ground contact around the edge of the boot sole) and instep crampons (typically provides four sharp points of ground contact at the middle of the boot sole—or instep).

Ranger Station:

What happens to the Colorado River in the winter? It is not uncommon for the river to support ice floes.

Ranger Station:

Does it snow at the bottom of the canyon? The bottom of the canyon sometimes receives a dusting of snow—and occasionally several inches.

The Inner Canyon will typically retain snow down through the timberline, while the remainder will melt while descending into the canyon and continue as sleet or rain. However, it is common for the Inner Canyon to receive a dusting of snow and sometimes several inches. In the winter of 1889–1890, Grand Canyon pioneer and Inner Canyon railroad surveyor Robert Brewster Stanton said of the canyon, *It has been the fortune of but few to travel along the bottom of the great chasm for a whole winter, while around you bloom sweet flowers ... and at the same time far above, among the upper cliffs, rage and roar the grandest storms of wind and snow.*

Photos by Flood Hefley

Alpine life zone. Upper Bright Angel Trail (above). Winter along the South Rim's Rim Trail, or "Greenway" (right).

Mines and Miners

Mining activity started in the late 1800s and remained at a high rate for only a short time. Asbestos, silver, zinc, uranium, vanadium, lead, and copper claims were filed. By the early 1900s, miners surrendered, as operations proved too costly. The dream of prospectors in the Grand Canyon was to achieve overnight wealth through gold strikes. Placer gold traces were discovered along the Colorado River, but because of the lack of technology, the specimens were too fine for profitable mining. **Copper Mining** began as early as 1875 and ceased by 1910. Like other Grand Canyon mining ventures, packing the ore out of the canyon and refining the 100 pounds of raw material that it took to produce one pound of pure copper proved too great a task and expense compared to the profit.

Grand Canyoneering: The first white man known to leave record of boat passage on the Colorado River System was the elusive Denis Julien. The French-Canadian fur trapper from St. Louis, Missouri, inscribed his name and date on cliff walls in Labyrinth Canyon, upstream from Grand Canyon. While on a "preinundation survey" of prehistoric and historic sites in Glen Canyon, archaeologist C. Gregory Crampton registered the inscription, *Ce Jan–1837*, "This January–1837." The mysterious Julien may have undertaken the Colorado River rapids in Grand Canyon. However, like a prospector protecting his claim, Julien left no evidence detailing the exact area of his endeavors, leaving a breech in history.

The Last Chance Mine of the Inner Canyon is 9 aerial miles southeast of the South Rim's El Tovar Hotel. The principal speculators, Pete Berry and the Camerons, Ralph and Niles, filed claims on and below Horseshoe Mesa in the Grand View area beginning in 1890. The claims were organized in 1895 as the Grand Canyon Copper Company. Copper ore was taken out of a half-mile of tunnels and shafts within seven levels. The ore was then packed to the South Rim by burros and mules and offloaded into wagons destined for Flagstaff, Arizona. Once at Flagstaff, the ore was transferred to rail cars and taken to outside markets, such as El Paso, Texas. At Chicago's 1893 Columbian Exposition, the ore was awarded as 70 percent pure. Ultimately, the cost of running such an operation in the late 1800s and early 1900s exceeded the earnings. After closing the mine, Berry turned to the business of tourism. Evidence of the mine remains in the forms of mine shafts, tools, and the ruined walls of "The Cook Shack."

Grand Canyoneering: The Lost John Doyle Lee Mine is speculated to be a gold deposit located at the bottom of the Tanner Trail. The discovery was made by ferry operator John Lee, circa 1886. In 1900, Grand Canyon pioneer William Bass sought the seven containers of gold that Lee allegedly hid in Havasu Canyon, 65 aerial miles west of the Tanner Trail. The mine and the gold remain hidden in the canyon—if it ever existed at all.

Today, it is important as a bat colony. In June 2007, thirty-nine **Townsend's big-eared bats** were observed emerging from the Last Chance Mine. In 2009, to protect this bat species, the mine entrance was outfitted with bat-friendly gating.

The Lost Orphan Mine is located 1,100 feet below Maricopa Point, 1 aerial mile west of the South Rim's El Tovar Hotel. Alternately called "The Orphan Mine," Daniel Hogan established the diggings to mine copper in 1893. Like every other early mining venture in Grand Canyon, the high cost of extraction from the remote and rugged terrain motivated Hogan to shift business endeavors to the up-and-coming tourism market. In Hogan's time, the new metallic element in his copper mine was not yet sought, so the mine lay dormant. The United States Geological Survey's discovery of **uranium** deposits in the Lost Orphan in 1951 prompted a revival of the mine. The site then operated under the Golden Crown Mining Company and later the Western Gold and Uranium Company. Residing 1,500 feet below the rim surface, the main deposit was carried out of the canyon by the aid of a three-tower aerial tram. The tram was later replaced by an 80-foot-high steel head frame, equipped with a hoisting shaft that remained historically on the 20-acre site until January, 2009. In 1962, Congress authorized the Secretary of the Interior to receive the site title. Even though mining activities were to cease no later than 1987, operations in Grand Canyon National Park concluded in 1969.

Head frame. Lost Orphan Mine, South Rim, 1963. The framework was removed when the site was restored to its natural state in 2009. GRCA 4220C

The Chuar Valley Mines, located 11 aerial miles southeast of the North Rim's Grand Canyon Lodge, were first prospected via mine shafts by Harry McDonald, who searched for copper and silver circa 1891. The mine was later renewed by the McCormick family. The ore was transported on the Tanner Trail near today's Indian Watchtower at Desert View.

Abandoned claim. The precarious entrance of the McCormick Mine. GRCA 5168

"Long" Tom Watson's story of gold starts in a letter that he discovered. The letter, dated 1909, included a map to a hiding place of gold in the eastern region of the canyon. The letter revealed that the nuggets were in a cave behind a Tanner Trail area waterfall. According to Watson, he found the gold in 1914. While bringing out some of the gold, the prospector suffered a near fatal injury that required an extended recuperation. When Watson returned to the canyon from Flagstaff, Arizona, the waterfall had dried up and he could not relocate the cave. The thought of the waterfall never flowing again and he not being able to ever relocate the gold defeated Watson. According to the story, the distressed Tom Watson took his life on the South Rim of the canyon.

Grand Canyoneering: In 1911, Charles Spencer utilized steam power to run his hydraulic mining operation in the region above Lees Ferry. Spencer stripped the cliffs down with high volumes of water through large diameter hoses. The material was then sluiced and the water returned to the Colorado River.

Ranger Station:
Is the Lost Orphan claim called "orphan" because it is an abandoned mine? Daniel Hogan, the patent holder, was an orphan who left New York in 1866 at age thirteen. Together with business partner Henry Ward, he staked the claim on the mine in 1893. Thus, the mine was commonly called the Lost Orphan Mine because Hogan was an orphan.

Ranger Station:
How was copper ore moved from the Last Chance Mine to the South Rim, and how much ore was shipped to market? The ore was removed from Horseshoe Mesa by mules and burros. A mule could handle 200 pounds of ore and made one trip per day. When there was an ample amount of material stockpiled on the South Rim at Grand View Point, it was then hauled to the nearest railroad stop, at Flagstaff, Arizona. In the time of commercial operation, a grand total of 140 railroad car-loads of copper ore were dispatched to El Paso, Texas, the nearest processing point.

The Fur Trappers, also called Mountain Men, used several points of entry into the 1820's West, such as Taos, New Mexico Territory. Others traveled the Gila River of the Arizona Territory, and the Green and Grand Rivers of the Utah Territory. The Grand Canyon was frequented by a scant few trappers, who searched primarily for beaver. The canyon was a barrier to such men as Jedediah Smith and James Ohio Pattie—and to others like Bill Williams and the mysterious French-Canadian Denis Julien. However, trapping did occur on the Colorado River and in places like Bright Angel Creek. Like miners protecting a claim, trappers protected their rich trapping sites and were unclear about locations. This tactic, while prudent for the time, provides little to no documented evidence of their travels in Grand Canyon.

Photo by Flood Hefley

Remote claim. Relics of the William Bass mining era, Shinumo Creek, Inner Canyon.

More—Did You Know?

Colin Fletcher hiked the length of the Grand Canyon in 1967. Fletcher, who was supplied by airdrops (no longer sanctioned) and provisions brought down trails, began in April on the trail to the Havasupai Indian Reservation in the western canyon. In June, he exited the eastern canyon on the Nankoweap Trail. The feat had never been attempted at the time, when Grand Canyon National Park was shorter and did not include the very rugged Marble Canyon and Toroweap regions.

A little horses scheme was uncovered in 1938 by Grand Canyon naturalist Edwin McKee and rangers Bert Lauzon and Warren Hamilton. Circuses were attracting patrons by exhibiting little horses that were "found in the Grand Canyon." The horses were advertised as stock that had become stunted after being cut off from normal grazing by a landslide. While McKee and the others did find small horses that were naturally small due to the meager grazing of the desert, in actuality, the horses were stunted Shetland ponies that were raised on a ranch.

Evel Knievel in 1967 proposed a 2-mile jump over the Grand Canyon's Marble Canyon on the rocket-based *Skycycle*. His plan was to launch from the Navajo Indian Reservation and land on the rim region of Marble Canyon. The United States government denied permission. In 1999, Knievel's son Robbie made a 228-foot jump near the terminal point of a narrow side canyon of the parent Quartermaster Canyon on Hualapai Indian Reservation land west of Grand Canyon National Park. After the scheduled jump was postponed due to snow and ice conditions, days later Robbie Knievel made the jump. However, he crash-landed on a poorly designed dirt landing strip.

Easter Sunrise Service at Mather Point has been offered consecutively since 1902.

The Grand Canyon Cowboy Band started in 1935 as a group of Fred Harvey Company employees, typically wranglers, who performed for South Rim and Phantom Ranch visitors.

Pastoral moment. Bull buffalo at House Rock Valley, 1949. GRCA 1862

"Cattalo" was the attempt made in 1907 to crossbreed buffalo. A collective herd of ninety buffalo were delivered to Lund, Utah, by railroad, and then driven through the Marble Canyon rim area of House Rock Valley to the Kaibab Plateau. Charles Jesse "Buffalo" Jones and "Uncle" Jim Owens, the Grand Canyon Game Reserve game warden, pastured the animals near Bright Angel Point and supplanted cattle to the herd. The outcome was an unprofitable hybrid. Today, a managed buffalo herd inhabits House Rock Valley.

Desert Varnish refers to the striations on the Redwall Limestone Formation cliff faces, which occur as a result of iron oxide, manganese, and various clays that wash down from the above strata.

Cache is from the French *cacher*, "to hide." Experienced hikers set aside equipment, water, and food on round-trip waterless trails for the return to the canyon rim. This maneuver alleviates hauling equipment and food down into the canyon that will not be used until the trip out. Hikers are reminded to use the animal proof containers provided in established campsites and to use an interlocking wire mesh bag when camping at large in the backcountry.

Inaugural run. The Atchison, Topeka and Santa Fe's "El Capitan" arriving at Grand Canyon Depot with its Leland A. Knickerbocker Native American headdress paint scheme, known as the "Warbonnet," seemingly bent by speed around the nose, February, 1938. GRCA 1318

Photo by Flood Hefley

On the ready. Rescue litter staged in the Mile-and-a-Half Resthouse, Bright Angel Trail.

Private livestock is limited to horses and mules. Rider-owners with a "livestock use permit" are restricted to the Bright Angel and Kaibab Trails. Since grazing is not permitted, sufficient quantities of feed must be packed. Personal safety and removal of injured or deceased livestock is the responsibility of the rider-owner.

Paul Bunyan, as told in the American tale, walked from North Dakota to California while dragging his axe with plowshare resistance. The axe made a crosscut through the sedimentary layers of Northern Arizona where the Grand Canyon was left to grow greater and greater in size by the Colorado River.

The Grand Canyon Trust was conceived in 1983 by boatman Martin Litton and conservationist Hughey Johnson, who formed the beginnings of the trust while on the Colorado River. The trust was established in 1985 as a non-profit organization with the goals to: *Identify and promote scientific, social, legal, and economic principals for conservation and sustainable management of the cultural and natural resources on the Colorado Plateau.* Grand Canyon National Park is located within the greater Colorado Plateau.

Index

(Italic page numbers indicate photographs)